EASY ENTERTAINING

With Jane Asher

EASY ENTERTAINING

With Jane Asher

Recipes by Jenny Alston

LONDON   NEW YORK   SYDNEY   TORONTO

Publisher's note All but two of the cake designs are based upon shop-bought cakes. The two exceptions appear on pages 20 and 56 and are based upon baking-tray cakes. Cross references in small capitals refer to topics discussed elsewhere in the book, the appropriate page number being given at the foot of the page against the given key word.

This edition published 1993
by BCA by arrangement with
Conran Octopus Limited

Originally published in 1987 by Conran Octopus Limited,
37 Shelton Street, London WC2H 9HN
Reprinted in 1988
Revised edition produced in 1991

Cookery consultant Jenny Alston
Editors Mary Davies, Patsy North
Contributing editors Emma Johnson-Gilbert and Mary Lambert
Art editor Caroline Courtney
Designer Caroline Murray
Original photography by Martin Brigdale
Photographic stylist Sue Russell
Food prepared for photography by Jacki Baxter
Colour illustrations by Flo Bayley
Black and white illustrations by John Woodcock
Production controller Michel Blake

CN 5507

Typeset by Vantage Photosetting Co. Ltd. and Hunters Armley
Printed and bound in Hong Kong

CONTENTS

INTRODUCTION

Away with panicking over sinking soufflés and soggy stuffings –
entertaining should be fun! There was a time when I would spend
hours in the kitchen, slaving over four or five courses for a dinner
party, and then go through the evening in a state of high tension,
worried about the timing of the food rather than enjoying the
company. The arrival of three delightful but time-consuming
additions to our household forced me to change: I can no longer
afford the luxury of hours spent boning pheasants or skinning
tomatoes. I still love to cook, but there are ways of making it
easier and quicker, especially for informal entertaining. And even
on the few occasions when I want to be more formal, I have
discovered over the years all sorts of tricks for making the evening
special and memorable while still managing to keep myself
relatively calm and happy.

In this book my aim is to share all that hard-earned experience!
I have roped in my good friend Jenny Alston to sort out some of
my favourite recipes and translate them into cook's English, and
she has added lots of marvellous ideas of her own – all of which
have been a delight to cook and taste while writing the book. But,
however good the food you serve, it won't be really appreciated
unless your setting is comfortable and appealing. Here, again, I've
picked my friends' brains and come up with a host of simple but
effective ideas for creating the right atmosphere.

All our food and presentation suggestions for special occasions
can be mixed and matched for many other celebrations. I hope you
will be inspired to use them in your own special way.

I have really enjoyed putting this book together. The whole team
of people who've played a part has been a delight to work with,
but I owe a special thanks to Tristram Holland, whose enthusiasm,
skill and friendship were a particular inspiration to me.

Jane Asher.

Plan ahead! This doesn't mean you have to work to a military plan of campaign with a six-month countdown. A simple list of what you have to do (and when) can put a stop to that feeling of being overwhelmed by all the little things that need to be arranged whenever you entertain. The more advance preparation you can do the better. Aim to complete one or more of the courses the day before, or at worst, early on the day. Your store cupboard and fridge/freezer can be your allies. A good supply of useful ingredients which really earn their keep can save time whenever you decide to entertain and will obviously reduce the panic of last-minute entertaining or the problem of feeding unexpected guests when all the shops are closed.

Stock cubes Keep a selection of chicken, beef, fish and vegetable stock cubes to use in soups and casseroles. Yeast extract, and tubes of vegetable and garlic pureé, are also good sources of extra flavour. You can make your own stock cubes if you like: boil stock in an uncovered pan until it is reduced in quantity by half; freeze in ice-cube trays, then store in a plastic bag in the freezer for up to a year.

Oils Olive, safflower and sunflower are particularly good for salads. Walnut and hazelnut are more expensive but make something special out of a few modest green salad leaves. Corn, soya and groundnut oils are good for frying and stir-frying, while sesame seed oil gives a superb flavour to oriental and Middle Eastern dishes.

Vinegars These are invaluable for salad dressings, and for marinades to tenderize meat. Wine vinegar can be added to casseroles instead of wine, giving the same flavour. Use white wine and cider vinegar for flavourings and dressings, and red wine vinegar for marinades and pickles.

Tomato purée Invaluable for adding concentrated flavour to pizza bases, pasta sauces, and casserole dishes. Refrigerate tins and tubes after opening.

Tinned tomatoes These can be used as the basis for a quick sauce (for pizza and pasta, or as a filling for baked potatoes or green vegetables). Reduce a tin of chopped tomatoes with 1 tablespoon red wine or red wine vinegar, until very thick, then add 1 tablespoon tomato purée and seasoning. This freezes well.

Bread Vacuum-packed half-baked loaves are excellent standbys for unexpected guests: few things are as inviting as the smell of hot, fresh bread. Melba toast, pumpernickel, and breadsticks go well with all sorts of starters, as do warmed pitta bread (which can be stored in the freezer). Use up stale bread by making and freezing your own breadcrumbs – useful as toppings, mixed with a little grated cheese, for baked vegetables, fish and chicken dishes, and fried in butter as a crisp topping for apple or other fruit purées. They will keep up to a month in the freezer. Toasted breadcrumbs are also useful for coating escalopes or fish; dry fresh breadcrumbs in the oven and store for a month or so in a screwtop jar. Croûtons can give a

dramatic lift to soups and salads. Make them either by frying in a mixture of oil and butter, or by brushing generously with melted butter and baking in a hot oven for 10 minutes until golden brown. Adding garlic and herbs to the oil gives extra flavour. Store in plastic bags in the freezer for up to a month.

Sugar Keep a vanilla pod in a jar of sugar to add subtle flavour to sweet dishes, such as cooked fruit and custards.

Pasta and rice If you often need to cook in a hurry, keep a supply of easy-cook rice, small pasta shapes and no-cook lasagne. Fresh pasta keeps in the freezer for 2–3 months.

Herbs Fresh herbs can be loosely packed in plastic bags and kept for several days in the fridge, and for up to 3 months in the freezer. Dried herbs keep for up to 6 months in airtight containers, away from light.

Spices Like dried herbs, they should be kept in airtight containers away from light.

Ground spices tend to lose their flavour and should only be kept for 2–3 months ; but whole spices can be kept for longer – grind them as you need them.

Bottled sauces Worcester and soy sauces add a distinct dash of flavour to sweet and sour dishes, stir-fry dishes and meat sauces. Oyster sauce and Chinese barbecue sauce (hoi sin) are also very useful in oriental cooking.

Pesto Home-made or bought, it's delicious and can be used in lots of ways: with Parmesan for an instant pasta sauce; added to mayonnaise for a dip; mixed into butter as a base for other sandwich fillings.

Mayonnaise A good bought variety kept in the fridge forms the base of many dressings: mix it with tomato purée or pesto, or mixed chopped herbs or crushed garlic for dips with prawns, eggs and vegetables. It's better than butter in sandwiches in hot weather.

Mustard, pickle and chutneys It is worth keeping a few really good or exotic ones, to make something special out of a meal of cold meat and salad, or bread and cheese.

Tinned goods There are some foods which really earn their place in a larder, especially for use in last-minute, unexpected entertaining: anchovies; sardines;

tuna and salmon for salads; crab, clams and shrimps for adding to more sombre fish dishes, as well as to make starters and salads; cannellini beans for quick casseroles; artichoke hearts, asparagus tips and mushrooms for starters, and as additions to a plain green salad; tinned red kidney beans, almost better than home-cooked ones and excellent as a starter with a little raw onion and ginger. I find the most useful tinned soups are: asparagus, which can also be used as a sauce for fish; lobster bisque, which one would never prepare oneself, and which makes a lovely rich sauce for a fish lasagne; consommé; game soup, which can also be used as excellent stock for casseroles; and French onion, which can make a meal in itself when served with toasted slices of French bread and cheese. I try to avoid tinned fruit but some types survive the process, tastewise at least, and could be used in BRÛLEES or PURÉES.

Fruit juice Concentrated frozen orange juice is one of the most versatile juices; 2 tablespoons added to any chicken dish – whether to a casserole, or to the stuffing for a roast bird – is delicious; it is also useful for sorbets, and for making juice for fruit salads.

Dried mushrooms and peppers Dried mushrooms (porcini and cèpes) have a much stronger flavour than fresh mushrooms and, once reconstituted (by soaking in warm water for 15 minutes), they can be made into a delicious pasta sauce or added to pizzas. They are also excellent in casseroles. Peppers can be used in much the same way.

Alcohol Red and white wine and sherry can be used to tenderize meats in marinades and can be added to fish or meat dishes for extra flavour. Spirits such as brandy, rum and Calvados are ideal for FLAMBÉED savoury and sweet food.

Milk and cream It's a good idea to keep cartons of long-life milk, or powdered milk, and long-life whipping cream for times when you suddenly run out. They are palatable in sauces and cooked dishes, and when well disguised with other flavours such as lemon or chocolate.

Nuts and grains Nuts can provide wonderful contrasts in texture and a delicious flavour to both sweet and savoury dishes. They are also an excellent source of protein for vegetarians. They are good roasted and sprinkled over salads and cooked vegetables as well as over fruit. In addition to walnuts and almonds, pistachio and cashew nuts, pine kernels, sunflower, sesame and pumpkin seeds keep for 3–6 months.

STOCKING THE FREEZER

I tend not to use mine for made-up dishes, but find it invaluable for stock (which keeps 3–4 months), bread (1 month), pastry (3 months), pancakes (1 month), butter (6 months), fresh cream (3 months) and, of course, ice-cream (2–3 months) and sorbets (1 week). If you live miles from a fishmonger, you might consider keeping some fish in the freezer: prawns and fish, such as Dover sole and turbot, are good for quick dinner-party dishes (follow the date-mark instructions).

Vegetables that freeze well are all kinds of beans (broad beans, French beans, green beans and runner beans), peas, and sweetcorn. Broccoli and spinach keep their flavour, but are best made into a purée. All vegetables keep for 1 year.

The freezer is also good for keeping emergency supplies of nuts, and coffee beans last longer if kept in the freezer (1 year).

PLANNING AHEAD

I always find it easier if I write a list of things to be done and tick them off as I go. If you are giving a formal dinner, or inviting lots of guests, then the effort of making a detailed list really pays off – it saves you worrying about what time to turn the oven up or down, when to take something out of the freezer, or whether you've got time to make a salad dressing.

First choose your menu
◆ Never bother with more than three courses, unless one is simply cheese.
◆ Plan around one course, usually the main one, unless you have a favourite spectacular starter.
◆ Make sure that at least one course can be prepared in advance.
◆ Try to vary the colours and textures of the courses, and avoid having dairy products in all of them.
◆ Check that you have all the crockery and cutlery you need, including small dessert forks if you need them.
◆ Check that all the components of a hot course can be assembled at the same time. (Roast potatoes and soufflés, for instance, need to be in a hot oven for at least 30 minutes just before they are served, so you couldn't warm plates in the same oven.)
◆ Check that all the ingredients are in season, or readily available.
◆ Check that you have enough space to store the prepared food; some will need to be in the fridge, some at room temperature.

Write a shopping list
Double check against each recipe, remembering all required garnishes and accompaniments (such as a special mustard).
◆ Check that you have all the 'store cupboard' ingredients you need.

Draw up a plan of action
Begin with the time your guests are due to arrive and work backwards.
◆ Remember to include time for tidying up the kitchen, changing, and 5 minutes to relax and admire your handiwork!
◆ Divide the list into things you can do a week or a day in advance and those that must be done on the day.
◆ Double check the list by mentally going through the whole evening, asking yourself these sorts of questions:

Drinks Are there ice-cubes and soft drinks to hand? Is the white wine in the fridge? Is the red wine open and at room temperature?
Table Have you planned the seating arrangements? Are there matches to light the candles?
First course Do you need to warm bread, or make toast?
Main course Are the plates warm? (Last-minute tip: hold them under very hot running water. Once hot, they are very quick and easy to dry.) Will the vegetables or a sauce need last-minute attention? If so, can you do this during drinks or can you slip out at the end of the first course?
Pudding Is the cream ready in a jug in the fridge? Does ice-cream need to be taken out of the freezer so that it is not rock-solid?
Cheese Is it laid out (with butter and biscuits to hand) at room temperature?
Coffee Have you ground the beans or measured out some ground coffee?

FOOD PRESENTATION

There is no question that the way food looks makes a dramatic difference to its taste. That may sound crazy, but imagine how unappetizing navy-blue fish would be. One of my great pleasures is presenting food attractively. By that I don't mean that fussy, finicky style of cooking which would have you labouring over the sculpting of a radish but I do enjoy working with pastry, for instance, and even the simplest shapes of puff pastry – fingers or crescents – make a nice alternative to bread as an accompaniment to soup or poached fish dishes. Brushed with egg yolk and sprinkled with caster sugar, they also make pretty crisp biscuits for soft fruit puddings. Even if my husband and I are eating alone I like to throw a bit of parsley and a lemon wedge next to the grilled fish. And when you're entertaining, it's fun to take a little extra trouble or add that element of surprise – anything from simply scattering crystallized rose petals on a lemon soufflé to colour co-ordinating your entire menu for an instant 'designer dinner'!

MAKING VEGETABLES LOOK GOOD

With a few extra minutes, it is easy to make vegetables more attractive.

Platters and gratin dishes help to show them off and they can be arranged very attractively in stripes and circles. Simply putting two varieties side by side on one dish, instead of in two, makes them look more interesting, as well as making them easier to serve.

Think of colour contrasts: a ring of dark green broccoli around a whole white cauliflower; chopped spinach piled inside a ring of mashed potato; alternate rows of green beans and sliced mushrooms; of blanched grated carrots and celeriac; or of red and white cabbage. Experiment with contrasting shapes too: peas and mange-tout; runner beans and broad beans.

A simple topping adds visual and textural interest too: raw carrot curls (made with a potato peeler); toasted, flaked almonds; tiny croûtons on purée; fried breadcrumbs or onion rings; spring onion brushes; a drizzle of sour cream and a generous sprinkling of chopped herbs.

ICINGS FOR CAKE DECORATION

Fondant icing Use it for covering cakes or for modelling. You can make your own fondant or buy ready-made 225 g ($\frac{1}{2}$ lb) blocks from supermarkets or delicatessens.

To make your own, use 1 egg white to 450 g (1 lb) sifted icing sugar and 1 tablespoon glucose liquid or syrup. Mix with a wooden spoon, form into a ball and, on a surface dusted with icing sugar, knead until pliable, adding a little water if necessary. Store in an airtight polythene bag in a cool place for up to 3 months. When needed, roll out onto a dusted surface and use at once; put the rest back in the bag immediately or it will dry out.

Food colouring Colour fondant icing by kneading in drops of food colouring, a little at a time; it can take a while for the colour to be evenly distributed. A variety of colours are available – gold and silver are non-toxic but don't eat them – I · don't anymore.

Royal icing Use it to cover cakes and to decorate. To cover a cake, use 250 g ($\frac{1}{2}$ lb) icing sugar to 1 egg white (more for piping). Mix it in a food processor, or with a wooden spoon. You can make it a week in advance and store until needed.

Buttercream For a 20 cm (8 in) sandwich cake use 75 g (3 oz) butter, 1 egg yolk, 450 g (1 lb) sifted icing sugar, 1 tablespoon milk or 1 egg yolk (or orange juice for a sharper taste). Beat the butter until soft and gradually beat in the icing sugar and the milk or egg.

Icing tubes and baking parchment All the cakes can be decorated using tube numbers 1, 2, 5 and 8. I used numbers 2 and 5 for plain piping; number 8 for shell borders and number 1 for lace on the VALENTINE CAKE. To make lace, slide your pattern under translucent baking parchment and trace the design with royal icing.

VALENTINE CAKE   **34**

MAKING AN ICE TRAY

An ice dish or tray looks spectacular and will keep ice-cream or sorbet cold long enough to serve second helpings. A sponge flan tin makes a perfect mould: simply fill with water and freeze overnight. You can tint the water with food colouring, or trap mint leaves in the rim.

FLOUR PASTE DECORATIONS

Tiny aspic cutters and children's templates offer a variety of shapes – you could also make wheatsheaves for THANKSGIVING – all lovely as table decorations.

Gradually mix water into plain flour, and knead until it is the consistency of plasticine. Bake the finished shapes at 300°F (150°C, gas mark 2) for 2 hours. The result is surprisingly durable. Paint with acrylic or gouache and varnish.

CRYSTALLIZED FLOWERS AND FRUITS

A sprinkling of frosted flowers or fruit can make something plain and simple look very special. Use small edible flowers – primroses, violets, freesia – or rose petals or mint leaves. They must be absolutely dry. Lightly beat an egg white with a pinch of salt; coat the flowers in egg, then in caster sugar, sprinkling more into the crevices. Shake off the excess and leave to dry in a warm dry place. Use the same method for grapes, red- or white-currants, and strawberries. They will keep for a week in an airtight jar.

COLOUR CO-ORDINATING YOUR FOOD

Make an ordinary occasion a little 'different', by planning everything around a colour theme, such as pink and black. Flowers, candles and table linen will state your theme most clearly, but you could even ask each guest to dress to match. The real test of your wit will be in the food you choose. Here are some suggestions.

Black Mussels, black olives, beans, bell peppers, nori (seaweed) parcels, grape-seed-coated cheese

Red Tomato soup, radicchio and radish salad, red peppers, tomato pasta, kidney beans, beetroot, pomegranates, plums, strawberries, raspberries

Pink Taramasalata, prawns, salmon mousse, beetroot-tinted rice, ham mousse, raspberry sorbet, rhubarb fool, Red Windsor cheese

White Almond soup, fish mousse, chicken breasts in white wine sauce, salsify, leeks, celeriac, lychees, lemon sorbet, meringue

Green Spinach roulade, watercress sauce, green beans, broccoli purée, mange-tout, spinach pasta, Sage Derby cheese, kiwi fruit, limes

Gold Pumpkin soup, glazed pastry, sweetcorn, yellow peppers and courgettes, smoked haddock, egg yolks, saffron rice, peaches, paw-paws, canteloupe melons

TABLE PRESENTATION

With very little extra time and expense you can make your table look stunning. Careful colour co-ordination is always wonderfully effective, but you can go for more 'theatrical' effects too – it doesn't matter if the decoration has lost its charm by the following morning. Don't despair if you're no great flower arranger – I'm certainly not. Experiment with simple but striking arrangements; it's much better than attempting something extremely elaborate that ends up making your room look like a hotel foyer gone wrong. Keep your lighting flattering and welcoming: don't forget candles. And how about doing something with those fairy lights that you stash away for eleven months of the year? We found a use for them at our VALENTINE BUFFET.

TABLECLOTHS, GARLANDS AND CENTREPIECES

A witty, pretty or dramatic table setting can do wonders when creating that special occasion atmosphere. A simple trick is to choose table napkins and candles that match the predominating colour of your china. Plain, dark colours are more dramatic, whereas the classic white and gold combination always looks sophisticated.

Go one step further – perhaps for a congratulatory or welcome-home party – and hang streamers from an overhead light which lead to each person's plate.

If you want to put two or more mismatched tables together for a large party, conceal the legs with an UNDERSKIRT. Or try using quantities of theatrical

muslin (which is really very cheap), gathered and stapled onto the back of sticky tape. Stick the tape around the perimeter of the tables, and top with a small overcloth. If you have to cheat with the overcloth, disguise a sheet with SCALLOPS secured by large safety pins. You can conceal the pins with bows of wide ribbon.

For a really grand occasion try making a garland – they're really easy to do. Take a stout cord the length of the required garland and make small loops at either end: the garland will be secured to the table with drawing pins. Working from one end of the cord, lay your chosen foliage along it (ivy is good,

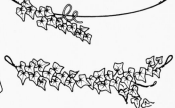

but mixtures of seasonal greenery are lovely too) and bind with florist's wire. You will probably have to add several layers, slightly staggered, to get the kind of thickness you want. Flower

heads bound into foliage often look wonderful too.

We suggest all sorts of CENTREPIECES in the book, including oyster-shell candles, floating candles and golden pasta dishes, but have you ever thought of having an edible centrepiece? There's our

jokey pears set-piece, for instance. Cored and seeded, the pears hold freesias at the start of the meal, but, at pudding time, invite your guests to help themselves (they can eat the freesias too, if they like!). Pass round a rich chocolate and nut pouring sauce.

IMPROVING YOUR LIGHTING

Good lighting can make a huge difference to the atmosphere. Of course people need to see what they are eating, but bright lights can be death to intimate conversation. Have a dimmer switch fitted to an overhead light if you can. Direct lighting is always harsh – a simple trick is to turn desk or spot lights to the ceiling to give an instantly softer light.

If you are eating in the kitchen, switch all lights off in the working areas so that the dinner table becomes the main focus of attention. Use a small table lamp on the worktop if you need to serve from there.

KEEPING CUT FLOWERS ALIVE LONGER

Strip off any leaves that will be in water (and take all the leaves off dahlias, lilac, chrysanthemums and mock orange). Then trim each stem at a slant so that as large an area as possible is exposed to the water. Woody stems of roses and flowering shrubs should be crushed or split at the base to help them absorb water. Adding a nutrient to the water can also help: a simple formula is an aspirin and a spoonful of sugar to a pint of water. Other nutrients are sold in florists, or you can buy a proprietary spray which prolongs vase life and prevents petals from drooping.

ARRANGING FLOWERS FOR THE TABLE

Unless your table is minute and absolutely anything extraneous would get in the way, flowers bring an immediate touch of class to any dinner table. You don't need to be a skilled florist or to spend a lot of time or money in order to create a distinctive or really pretty arrangement. The secret is simplicity, using the right containers and a little basic equipment.

If you can, keep to a single colour which complements the rest of your table setting. White is a safe bet, and always very elegant; it complements any colour. A spray of gypsophila makes a few other flowers go further.

A centrepiece shouldn't interfere with conversation. There's nothing worse than having to crane one's head round a huge bunch of flowers to talk to the person opposite. So keep the arrangement low. One very easy yet dramatic idea is to remove the stems of, say, large daisies completely and arrange the flowerheads in a simple, flat dish; stripes of different colours can look marvellous.

Pinholders are invaluable in keeping flowers – and especially those with woody stems – in place in a fairly upright arrangement; also worth seeking are the more old-fashioned glass holders as they look marvellous sitting in something as simple as a glass fruit-bowl. Vases with a broad lip are also very useful because the lip stops flowers tipping out and enables you to show off their faces.

Plastic foam, usually sold under the brand name Oasis, can be cut into blocks and will hold flowers at any angle so that you can even use something like a saucer for a centrepiece. But the foam must be soaked through or it will float and it must be concealed. You can make a very cheap but effective centrepiece by pushing three candles into some Oasis and disguising the surrounding foam with firm stemmed leaves.

It is much easier to arrange flowers in several small vases rather than in one large one. Cut the stems short and pop a few flowers in each one. You can use almost any container from old jars to fine crystal. A collection grouped together makes the most impact.

The dark-blue church glasses shown here were collected by Fleur Cowles and are used to great effect with a variety of flowers in a single colour. Or you could try putting a large single flower or tiny posy in a little vase or glass next to each place setting.

INFORMAL ENTERTAINING

This is the type of entertaining that most of us want to do most of the time: a few friends round for a meal in a relaxed atmosphere, and yet with that special touch in the food and setting that shows you've taken trouble. Most important of all is to prepare as much as possible the day or morning before, so that you, as well as your guests, can enjoy the evening.

Starters especially can often be made well ahead of time. Don't, however, be tempted to put them out on the table too early if they are likely to lose their sparkle, especially in warm weather. Your guests may be later than you think or 'drinks' may last longer than planned (it's easy to be side-tracked by the talk if it's good), and chilled soups or salads are not much fun served tepid or droopy.

However little time you have to prepare, make sure you lay the table before people arrive so things appear to be under control and you can sit down for a drink and chat before dinner rather than have to keep leaping up and down. Add some decoration to the table – it needn't be elaborate, a few flowers can work wonders – or even combine food and decor and go for an edible centrepiece. At a friend's house I recently enjoyed a clever, simple starter: a beautiful bowl of whole, raw vegetables was placed like some splendid still-life in the middle of the table, while before each guest was set a selection of dips, together with a sharp knife to cut off chunks of whatever vegetable took one's fancy.

You could go for an unusual, elaborate starter and then play down the main course. It's a good idea not to attempt a culinary breakthrough at every stage of the meal, but a little showing off at the beginning can set a good mood. Alternatively you could leave out a starter altogether and go for something filling with the pre-dinner drinks, especially if your guests' arrival times are likely to be staggered.

Don't worry too much about getting the house perfect: people will enjoy themselves just as much if you haven't managed to polish the dachshund or remove all evidence of human habitation – the odd toy lying around won't destroy your reputation as a hostess.

Right Clockwise from the left: *Grilled artichoke heart with Mozzarella; soup with Puff-pastry top; Spinach roulade with curried prawn filling (page 104); Marinated Brie (page 90). For the grilled artichoke, put a thick slice of tomato, a teaspoon of tomato sauce and some Mozzarella onto a round of pumpernickel and grill. For the* *pastry top, brush the rims of the heatproof soup bowls with beaten egg yolk, press rolled-out puff pastry into place on top, brush with egg yolk and bake in the oven until risen and golden; it is best served with clear vegetable soup and followed with a cold main course as it must be cooked in a high oven (450°F, 230°C, gas mark 8) for 20 minutes.*

CRUDITÉS AND DIPS

One of the nicest, easiest appetizers is a selection of fresh raw vegetables to dip into hummus, taramasalata, HERB MAYONNAISES or DIPS. For a blue-cheese dip simply blend 225 g ($\frac{1}{2}$ lb) quark and 120 g (4 oz) blue cheese, and add a few drops of tabasco. Carrots, peppers and courgettes make good scoops; so do cauliflower florets, mushrooms, baby sweetcorn and celery.

SUPPER IN 90 MINUTES

Artichoke hearts with Mozzarella (*left*)
or
Spinach roulade
(*page 104*)

◆

Sweet and sour baked pork (*page 117*)
Braised spring onions
(*page 125*)
Party rice (*page 124*)

◆

Apple square puffs
(*page 133*)

The main course is often the base upon which you plan your menu. You won't want to spend all day hunting down smoked mongoose so choose something for which you know all the ingredients will be readily available and, again, prepare in advance as much as possible. Don't attempt anything too ambitious unless you've cooked it before, and be aware of any religious or dietary considerations among your guests: there's nothing more depressing than having to face a last-minute boiled egg.

It's often difficult to time your vegetables so that they are perfectly *al dente*, so why not BRAISE or PURÉE them instead? They are delicious either way and can be kept hot in the oven. One cooked vegetable may be enough – a SALAD could replace the second.

VEGETARIAN
SUPPER
PREPARED IN
ADVANCE

Marinated Brie
(page 90)

◆

Vegetable crumble
(page 120)
Tomato sauce
(page 139)

◆

Spicy apple meringue
(page 132)

SUPPER
MOSTLY PREPARED
IN ADVANCE

Watercress soup
(page 95)

◆

Pork and apricot
casserole *(page 119)*
Leek and potato purée
(page 126)
Green vegetable

◆

Stuffed pears with
chocolate sauce
(page 132)

SUPPER
MOSTLY PREPARED
IN ADVANCE

Taramasalata *(page 81)*

◆

Greek beef casserole
(page 114)
Plain rice or noodles

◆

Apple topsy-turvy
(page 130)

SUPPER
IN 90 MINUTES

Paella *(page 100)*
or
Four cheese pasta
(page 106)
Choice of salads
(pages 82–3)

◆

Fruit brûlée *(page 86)*

Right Clockwise from the left: *one-dish main courses – Greek beef casserole (page 114), sprinkled with feta cheese for melting in the oven; Paella (page 100) – which is also good* *served straight from a paella pan; Vegetable crumble (page 120); Pork and apricot casserole (page 119).*

Here's another chance to make something a little special that can be prepared ahead of time. Instead of a straightforward fruit pie, try a delicious apple topsy-turvy; instead of pancakes, elegant crêpes, which can either be made in advance or cooked in front of your guests and then filled with any one of a number of delicious concoctions. Or make a refreshing FRUIT SALAD with some of the exotic tropical fruits now available at any season in so many supermarkets. For speedy puddings try bought sorbets — they can be really good; look out particularly for those made with pure ingredients. It's worth buying an ice-cream scoop to make the servings attractive.

If you want to have cheese, you can either serve it before the pudding, in the French style, or keep it for afterwards as the English do: whichever you decide, it's better to go for two or three large pieces rather than a vast selection of little bits. Don't spurn the humbler cheeses — a really good piece of Cheddar cut off the block is still one of the greats, and far better than a pre-packed chunk of something supposedly more exotic.

You could leave out a pudding altogether and just team your cheese with fresh fruit, especially if the meal has been heavy. A large slab of ripe Brie alongside a generous bunch of black grapes looks stunning and tastes marvellous; Stilton and pears is another winning combination.

FILLINGS FOR SWEET CRÊPES

Crêpes can be made in advance and stored (unfilled) in the freezer between layers of greaseproof paper or foil. Serve with any of these fillings.

◆ Dried fruit cooked in honey and lemon juice

◆ Peach and pear in almond crème patissière, dusted with icing sugar and served with RASPBERRY PURÉE

◆ Banana and almonds with brown sugar and coffee sauce

◆ Oranges and dates, flambéed with brandy

◆ Apple and Calvados with whipped cream and ice-cream

◆ Toasted pine kernels, apricot jam and apricot or orange liqueur

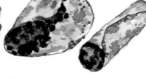

SUPPER
IN 60 MINUTES

Bœuf stroganoff
(page 114)
Party rice *(page 124)*
Steamed courgettes
or
Choice of salads
(pages 82–3)
◆
Fruit clafoutis
(page 131)

Right Clockwise from the left: *selection of baked desserts – Fruit clafoutis (page 131); Spicy apple meringue (page 132), decorated with whole blanched almonds; Apple topsy-turvy (page 130), made in a heart shape; Plum crumble (page 133), sprinkled with flaked almonds.*

Sometimes it's fun to surprise everyone with a showy masterpiece at the end of the meal. At Christmas time you're expected to set the pudding on fire and enter dramatically to cries of 'oooh' and 'aaaaah' but why limit it to Christmas? Cut a dash at other times too, and have fun with sparklers and decorations. I first came across sparklers as food decoration when I saw them thrust into a pudding in Greece, but they also look wonderful in individual goblets of ice-cream – especially appreciated by any children present.

Baked Alaska used to be one of my mother's stand-bys for dinner parties – but it never looked like this! I was always intrigued by the magic of cold ice-cream inside hot meringue and it still gives me a sense of occasion whenever I eat it. Served with sparklers as a surprise ending to a celebratory meal, it could make your guest of honour feel very special. 'Happy Birthday' could well be sung round a sparkling baked Alaska – and there would be no need to count the candles!

A home-made cake is also a traditional way of marking an occasion, not just a birthday but any time when you want to make someone feel especially loved. It mustn't look as if it's come from a cake shop, so try to make it as personal as possible and decorate it to suit your theme, as with our 'Bon Voyage' suitcase.

LUSCIOUS COFFEES

A delicious alcohol-laced coffee makes a marvellously mellow end to a meal.

◆ **Gaelic coffee:** made with 1 measure Scotch whisky, coffee and sugar (optional). Stir the coffee fast until it is spinning, and then trickle double cream over the back of a spoon onto the top. The layer of cream should remain on top of the coffee.

◆ **Irish coffee:** made in the same way, but with Irish whiskey instead of Scotch.

◆ **Coffee brûlot:** made by adding some crushed cinnamon and cloves, julienne strips of orange and lemon rind and 1 teaspoon sugar to 1 measure brandy and 1 teaspoon Curaçao. Stir until the sugar dissolves. Light the brandy and gradually add the hot coffee until the flame goes out.

Right *Serve a 'sparkling' Baked Alaska as an alternative to a birthday cake. You can omit the ice-cream but the classic Alaska is a sponge flan filled with ice-cream and piled high with meringue. Cover the sponge and ice-cream completely with meringue – 225 g (½ lb) caster sugar to 4 egg whites, whisked together – and bake in a hot oven for just 2–3 minutes, or for 10–15 minutes at a lower temperature if you are omitting the ice-cream. If you are using ordinary sparklers, place a circle of foil at least 30.5 cm (1 ft) in diameter beneath the cake to catch the sparks; indoor cocktail sparklers are preferable. Don't use more than four of either type and get someone to help you light them simultaneously. They only last for a couple of minutes and there's a danger they'll go out before you reach the table. If you can warm them (carefully!) first, they will catch fire more quickly.*

SUITCASE CAKE

2 × 20 × 30 cm (18 × 12 in) sponge cakes; apricot jam; 8 × 225 g (½ lb) packets FONDANT ICING, coloured brown; silver and black FOOD COLOURING; non-toxic crayons; 2 sheets rice paper

Sandwich the cakes with jam and spread jam thinly over the top and sides. Cut fondant pieces for the sides of the 'case' and a rectangle for the 'lid', allowing a 4 cm (2 in) overlap all round. Attach the sides to the cake, then the lid, smoothing down the overlap and trimming to join the corners. Model and secure a handle and fastenings. Colour the fastenings silver. Cut out and attach rice-paper stickers with fondant, and finally draw black stitches around the lid.

Just occasionally it's fun to give a more formal dinner party. Few of us nowadays have butlers, parlourmaids, cooks and footmen to run our houses, but a little bit of tongue-in-cheek grandeur can make a special occasion even more memorable.

Not only the food you choose but also the way you lay the table can give a sense of style to a meal. If, like me, you don't have one of the vast, beautiful damask cloths of old, a clever trick for covering the table is to put a large sheet over it which comes almost down to the ground and add a small cloth on top. This will look suitably formal, and, if you put a thin blanket on the table first, you won't need mats and you'll have given the cloth a sumptuous, padded feel. Matching the colour of the napkins to your cloth is always very effective; real ones are wonderful but, if you have to use paper napkins, then go for the slightly thicker type that feels like fabric.

Lighting is crucial; a bright overhead light can wreck any feeling of intimacy and relaxation – and most rooms benefit from soft, flattering side-light, as do most people. If you choose candles, make sure the guests can see what they're eating; I've been in some dimly-lit restaurants where I wasn't sure if I was about to eat lamb chops or poached pears. Don't worry if you haven't got many candlesticks – you can improvise any number of ways of securing a candle,

Right *If you don't have a grand dining room, a group of candles on the mantelpiece or a high shelf give a soft-focus light to the room and festive feel to the occasion. Cover the mantelpiece or shelf with a sheet of foil to catch drips and place candles in dishes or candlesticks. If you have a mirror above the mantelpiece, the reflection of candlelight will double the effect.*

NAME CARDS

Name cards add friendly formality to the table and stop guests lingering awkwardly in the doorway. A simple design can be drawn on white card. Mark a dotted line horizontally across the middle of a piece of card and draw a simple shape (a bow tie or flower, perhaps) that is bisected by the line. Cut out the upper half of the shape, fold the card along the dotted line and push the cut section upright. Add a guest's name and the card is ready. For festive occasions, add colour or glitter.

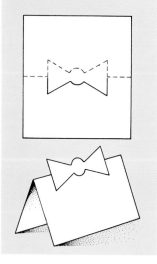

PLACE SETTINGS FOR A FORMAL TABLE

A table looks more formal with lots of cutlery: a chance to use fish knives and forks and fruit forks if you have them. Arrange cutlery in the order it will be used, working from the outside inwards with the sharp edges of knife blades facing inwards. Apparently the tips should point to the appropriate glass for each course but frankly I'm not too worried about such detail. Don't forget to lay serving spoons, and spoons and ladles for sauces and creams. If you are serving red and white wine – or wine and port – have glasses for each. The one for red wine should preferably be larger than that for white, and don't forget a water glass.

OYSTER CANDLES

Oyster shells make very pretty and unusual candles, their undersides perhaps painted to match a colour theme. Buy candle wax and wicks, weighted with a disk at one end, from a craft shop. Trim each wick till it's 6.3 cm (2½ in) long and place the weighted end in the shell. Holding the other end of the wick upright, pour in the melted wax and wait until it has set.

Left Clockwise from the left: *Broccoli purée (page 126); Chicken filo pie (page 110); julienne of carrots; Layered avocado and tomato mousse (page 91).*

DINNER PREPARED IN ADVANCE

Layered avocado and tomato mousse
(page 91)

◆

Chicken filo pie
(page 110)
Broccoli purée
(page 126)
Glazed carrots

◆

Champagne sorbet
and/or
Cranberry and port
sorbet *(page 128)*

DINNER IN 120 MINUTES

Cream of scallop soup
(page 95)

◆

Roast meat or poultry
Herbed garlic potatoes
(page 123)
Braised leeks *(page 125)*
Green vegetable

◆

Flambéed fruit *(page 86)*

Left Clockwise from the left: *White chocolate mousse with dark chocolate sauce (page 129); Champagne sorbet (page 128); Cranberry and port sorbet (page 128); Pancake-wrapped peaches (page 131).*

and it's much more effective to group them than to scatter them singly.

As for the food: a formal meal is the chance to do something showy – it doesn't have to be complicated to produce, but the end result must look as if you cared enough to take a little trouble. Our suggested menus are designed to banish last-minute panics. If the menu you have chosen is new to you and you have the time, it's worth having a complete rehearsal a few days before; you don't have to use identical ingredients – substitute cod for salmon for your practice run, for instance. Check on your guests' likes and dislikes – if you're buying expensive ingredients, you certainly don't want them pushed discreetly to the side of the plate. I don't think it's worth spending hours turning a turnip into a rose, or a carrot into the Eiffel Tower, but do take a little extra trouble over the presentation. If you decide to have a cheese course, serve it before or after the pudding, and a sorbet can be used in the classic French way to both clear and refresh the palate between courses.

Make sure you allow yourself plenty of time to get ready. If you've asked your guests to be dressy, you'll want to take some special care over your own appearance too. You don't want the doorbell to go while you're luxuriating in a well-earned bath.

DINNER
MOSTLY PREPARED
IN ADVANCE

Duck breast salad with
blackcurrant sauce
(page 90)

◆

Fish en croûte *(page 99)*
Watercress sauce
(page 139)
Choice of salads
(pages 82–3)

◆

White chocolate
mousse with dark
chocolate sauce
(page 129)

Above *Fish en croûte (page 99); Duck breast salad with blackcurrant sauce (page 90); curly endive and radicchio; oyster-shell candles (page 23).*

GRAND CELEBRATION DINNER

As long as you've got the space, a sit-down meal is somehow much more festive than a buffet, and it's surprising just how many you can squeeze in if you plan carefully. There are many occasions, lots of them family celebrations, when it's necessary to feed a large number of people in this way and it's marvellous if you can do it at home, instead of hiring an anonymous hotel or restaurant. Everything we've done here could be adapted to suit a variety of occasions, using almost any colour you like for your chosen theme.

We picked a golden wedding anniversary as a wonderfully happy and special milestone to celebrate! Nowadays it's impressive when people manage to be married for even ten years . . . especially to the same person. To reach fifty years surely deserves a party! At a time like this you can afford to go right over the top – get yourself a can of gold spray-paint and go to town.

There are likely to be relatives around for this sort of occasion so involve as many as possible in the preparations, delegating any tasks you can. Hire or borrow spare tables

Right *Gold trimmings, carefully placed, can really add that finishing touch to a table laid for a golden wedding celebration. Use gold candles, and place some gold net and white flowers along the middle of the table to make a pretty centrepiece. Place pasta-bow cards at each setting and wind some gold ribbon around the chairs to give a really festive feel to the dinner.*

HOT DINNER
FOR 24

Tuna roulade *(page 104)*

◆

Chicken and orange parcels *(page 113)*

◆

Lime and orange syllabub in dark chocolate shells *(page 130)*

HOT DINNER
FOR 12

Mushroom or prawn croûtes with drinks *(page 88)*

◆

Beef with dried wild mushrooms *(page 115)*
Parsnip and pear purée *(page 126)*
Green vegetable

◆

Champagne sorbet *(page 128)*

COLD DINNER
FOR 24

Canapés *(pages 36–7)*

◆

Cold poached salmon *(page 31)*
Mange-tout and pea salad *(page 127)*
New potatoes with cucumber dressing *(page 127)*
Choice of salads *(pages 82–3)*

◆

Amaretto mousse *(page 129)*

FOIL-PARCEL FOOD

◆ **Baked halibut** Cook rice as for Party rice *(page 124)* but simmer for only 10 minutes. Divide among the parcels and add 2 tablespoons cooked spinach to each. Lay 175 g (6 oz) fish on the spinach and dot with butter and ground fennel. Add a few shrimps, 1 tablespoon white wine and lemon juice. Season, seal and cook at 350°F (180°C, gas mark 4) for 20 minutes.

◆ **Pork chops** For each parcel, thinly slice 2 potatoes lengthways, season and dot with butter. Trim fat off the chop and lay the chop on the potato. Add 1 chopped red pepper to the Sweet and sour pork sauce *(page 117)*. Spoon 2 tablespoons over meat, seal and cook at 375°F (190°C, gas mark 5) for 45 minutes.

and chairs if necessary, covering tables with underskirts to disguise any strange-looking legs. Make up any missing glasses or cutlery by hiring or borrowing from a friend. You could hire the lot but don't worry if everything isn't perfectly matched; you can easily achieve a generally co-ordinated look by tying ribbons round the glasses or filling them with wrapped chocolates.

Don't forget place cards – you won't want to stand at the head of the table with a seating-plan in your hand, shouting directions as people come in. And, if there are family guests, do make sure they get on with their neighbours – don't sit great uncle Arthur next to cousin Harriet if they haven't been on speaking terms for over thirty years.

The food must be easy – when you're feeding really large numbers you don't want to be boning and stuffing frogs' legs or peeling 150 grapes. Here a relatively modern invention comes into its own – cooking foil. Not only does it suit our colour theme but the individually wrapped serving has advantages. You can judge the quantities exactly, there will be no time wasted doling out portions, and the food will keep warm and will not dry out. We've listed only a few possible fillings: experiment a few days before with some of the fresh ingredients in season. If you decide to go for a large ham or bird instead, it's much easier to carve it ahead and keep it warm.

Above *Chicken and orange parcels (page 113) and Roulade with tuna filling (page 104).*
Right *Golden wedding cake, and Lime and orange syllabub (page 130) in dark chocolate shells.*

COLD DINNER
FOR 12

Chilled cucumber soup with prawns *(page 94)*

◆

Tricolour fish mousse *(page 99)*
or
Chicken in walnut sauce *(page 109)*
New potatoes with cucumber dressing *(page 127)*
Choice of salads *(pages 82–3)*

◆

Pavlova *(page 130)*

HOW TO MAKE A GOLDEN PASTA DISH

A golden plate filled with sweets, truffles, biscuits or small cakes makes a stunning centrepiece. All you need is a plate, a ring base, spray paint, household glue and some pasta shapes (shells, nibs, spirals or bows). If you can find a ready-made polystyrene ring for the base, tremendous! If not, a sponge tin covered with foil works just as well. Cover the outside and inside of the tin with foil. Scrunch up another length of foil and bend it over the edge of the tin. Cover the whole thing with more foil to secure it. Brush glue all over the ring shape, and stick on a variety of pasta pieces. Spray with gold paint.

Individual pasta bows can also decorate NAME CARDS.

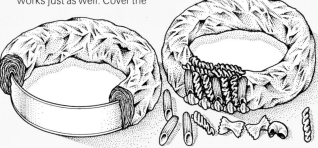

GOLDEN WEDDING CAKE

1 round fruit or sponge cake – 25 cm (10 in) deep; 3 × 225 g ($\frac{1}{2}$ lb) packets FONDANT ICING, coloured yellow; 1 × 225 g ($\frac{1}{2}$ lb) packet white fondant; gold FOOD COLOURING; 450 g (1 lb) ROYAL ICING

Roll out yellow fondant and cover the cake. Roll out the white fondant and from it cut the numbers – a large set for the top of the cake and six smaller sets to go round the side. Paint the numbers with gold colouring and stick onto the cake with a little royal icing. Trim the edges of the cake with decoratively piped royal icing, using a large shell nozzle. Pipe a large bow above the figures on top of the cake with a smaller shell nozzle and add some swirls below the figures.

SUMMER BUFFETS

A stand-up, indoor buffet is a good way to entertain large numbers of friends. Everyone can mingle freely and there's less chance of anyone getting stuck with the same companions all evening. But remember, people won't be less hungry just because it's not a sit-down meal, and a few 'bits on sticks' won't do.

The aim is to provide a reasonably substantial meal which can be eaten with one hand while standing up. We've all experienced the challenge of struggling to cut a slice of beef with the side of a fork while balancing a glass of wine and trying not to lose the thread of a complicated conversation. Paper plates are pretty hopeless as they tend to bend and go soggy; it's much better to hire or borrow china ones. You probably won't serve a starter but you could pass round a few CANAPÉS (a word I really hate) while guests are arriving. For your main course choose a cold centrepiece that can be prepared ahead and complete it with a variety of salads or tiny BAKED POTATOES. Summer fruit is so delicious that you can't go wrong with a large bowl of strawberries or raspberries.

You must rope in plenty of help with preparation and serving. Plan how people will approach the food table, putting the plates at the beginning and cutlery at the other end. Serve the wine as far from the food as possible to avoid the two queues getting mixed up and make sure you have enough bottles open for people to be able to get their first drink quickly. Buy plenty of ice from the supermarket or wine merchant; as your fridge will probably be full of food you'll need the ice for cooling the wine – in the bath if nothing else suggests itself.

It's worth taking trouble over the presentation of the meal: summer GARLANDS and pretty napkin rings are really very easy to make and they add so immeasurably to the atmosphere that they are well worth the relatively little extra preparation time they take.

SUMMER NAPKIN RINGS

Make pretty napkin rings for a summer table.

◆ A simple daisy chain or two, made with the daisy heads as close together as possible, and spare stalks trimmed off

◆ A long leaf (bay, willow, or laurel) secured by piercing the leaf with its stem or with a pin

◆ A knot of long grasses

COLD SUMMER BUFFET

Tricolour fish mousse
(page 99)
or
Poached salmon *(below)*
Cold meat platter
◆
Green pea and ginger
salad *(page 127)*
New potatoes with
cucumber dressing
(page 127)
Three-leaf salad
(below)
Pasta and nut salad
(page 106)
◆
Pavlova *(page 130)*

Left Clockwise from left: *Three-leaf salad of endive, radicchio and chicory; Pasta and nut salad (page 106); New potatoes with cucumber dressing (page 127); Green pea and ginger salad (page 127); Pimms; Pavlova (page 130) with raspberries and kiwi fruit; delicately tinted Tricolour fish mousse (page 99), made in a fish mould.*

COLD POACHED SALMON

Make a bouillon with the juice of 1 lemon, 3 glasses white wine, 1 teaspoon salt, 12 peppercorns and a bouquet garni. Lay the salmon flat in a fish kettle or curved in a large roasting pan. Pour over the bouillon, and top up with cold water to cover the fish. Bring to a boil and cook for 2 minutes. Turn off the heat and leave, covered with a lid or foil, until cold before serving.

WINTER BUFFETS

Mulled wine steaming gently in an earthenware jug, friends stamping snow off their feet as they enter the warmly-lit hallway, plates of piping hot food enjoyed amid laughter and song – the images of entertaining in winter are almost Dickensian. Make your setting as welcoming as possible: remember you may be deceptively warm from slaving in the kitchen so be sure the room temperature is high enough for your guests. If you notice one of them eating in an overcoat, you'll know you've misjudged it.

Hot food can be hard to organize for large numbers and it's essential that it can be kept warm for some time, so a casserole is almost certainly best. And it's easy to eat with a fork. (Basic principles don't differ from those laid down for SUMMER BUFFETS.) You could have a cold main course, as long as you have some hot vegetable accompaniment, and do allow plenty of food for everyone – people really need stoking up in the wintertime!

MULLED WINE AND NON-ALCOHOLIC PUNCH

Whether in a hut halfway up a mountain, or a town-house hallway, there's nothing as welcoming as mulled wine. Two bottles of full-bodied red wine and 300 ml (½ pint) water make 10 cups. Don't make too much at a time as it cools quickly, but if you have a slow cooker, leave the mixture on a low heat and add wine and sugar as needed.

Heat the wine and water with 2 tablespoons brown sugar, 1 stick cinnamon, 1 teaspoon grated nutmeg and slices of orange and apple (add 6 cloves if you like). Cook for 10 minutes to reduce and leave to infuse for 5 minutes. Add 110 ml (4 fl oz) brandy (optional), strain and reheat gently.

Make a warm non-alcoholic punch with 600 ml (1 pint) apple juice, 300 ml (½ pint) water, rind of 2 lemons, cinnamon, nutmeg and cloves to taste, and 6 tablespoons sugar.

HOT WINTER BUFFET

Cream cheese and herb dip *(page 88)*

◆

Beef with dried wild mushrooms *(page 115)*
Rice and potato nut balls *(page 123)*
Crispy potato skins with sour cream *(page 123)*
Glazed carrots

◆

Amaretto mousse *(page 129)*
Vienna biscuits *(page 134)*
and/or
Pumpkin pie *(page 133)*
Apple purée

Left *A winter table centrepiece combines grapes, evergreen foliage and coloured candles, attached with wax. If you don't have a silver dish, use a cake stand or glass bowl.*
Right *Crispy potato skins with sour cream (page 123); Beef with wild mushrooms (page 115); Rice and potato nut balls (page 123).*

There will be times when you want to serve a buffet that can be eaten with fingers – a more casual way of providing food for large numbers, and useful for the occasions when you don't have enough plates and cutlery to go round. Choose food which can be prepared ahead and served hot or cold: it's good to have some of each. It shouldn't be too difficult to handle – people tend to wave things around when talking, and the last thing you want is asparagus tips landing on a friend's new white outfit.

We've chosen Valentine's Day as a wonderful excuse for such a party, and you can make it as romantic and silly as you like. Our theme would also be a marvellous way to celebrate an engagement. It's worth setting aside some time to decorate the room as it'll help create the right atmosphere. Cover tables with thick paper cloths, stencilled with hearts, kisses and cupids: a pretty way to protect tables if you don't want to get rings on them. Even the food reflects our theme: buy a heart-shaped cutter and you can turn almost anything into a Valentine. A celebratory cake is always a good centrepiece, but you must be able to eat it without a fork and a plate.

Get help with the preparations – children would love to join in the stencilling – and also for the serving. Leave yourself something to hand around though as it can be a good way of helping guests to mingle.

CINNAMON HEARTS

You could tie pretty bows in the centre of individual Cinnamon hearts *(page 134)* instead of threading them all onto ribbon. Make two holes in each biscuit before baking, and pierce the holes again gently with a skewer before they cool. They'd look lovely hung on a Christmas tree. Try other shapes too – you can buy a variety of cutters.

VALENTINE CAKE

1 deep, round sponge cake – 20 cm (8 in) – cut into heart shape; BAKING PARCHMENT; 450 g (1 lb) white ROYAL ICING; 2 × 225 g ($\frac{1}{2}$ lb) packets FONDANT ICING, coloured red

Trace the lace pattern (below) onto baking parchment and pipe about 90 white shapes. Pipe a white arrow onto cardboard in two parts (head and flight). Cover the cake with red fondant and decorate the edges with royal icing. Using royal icing to secure, position the lace and arrow sections. Link the latter with a piped heart and lace.

BAKING PARCHMENT	10
ICING	10

Left *Valentine's Day is a good excuse for going over the top: light the table with fairy lights inside red plastic tulips.*

FINGER FOOD

Prawn croûtes with
creamy topping
(page 88)
Cheese biscuits

◆

Tandoori chicken
drumsticks *(page 111)*
Baked potatoes with
cheese and herbs
Chicory and radicchio
salad boats *(page 47)*

◆

Cinnamon hearts
(page 134)
Valentine cake
(opposite)

HEART TEMPLATE

On folded card (using a jar
as a guide), draw a circle
which just touches the fold.
Measure its diameter and
mark the fold that same
distance below the circle.
Join this mark to the other
side of the circle. Cut round
the heart outline and unfold
to complete the template.

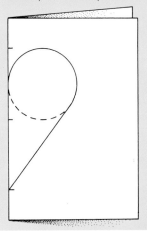

The old-fashioned image of a cocktail party is rather Noël Coward: elegant ladies in long, black dresses gesticulating with long, black cigarette holders while sipping something mysteriously green in tiny, tapered glasses. Nowadays we tend to think more in terms of a drinks party, which can mean anything from a keg of beer and some sausages to champagne and little rolls of smoked salmon.

The first decisions to make are how many people to invite and just how formal it will be. Your answers will determine the type of food and drink you serve. A choice of red and white wine or Buck's Fizz is fine for most occasions or, if there are not too many people, why not serve cocktails? I love them and they do lend a certain glamour. Alternatively a MULLED WINE, PUNCH or WINE CUP can be fun. Do remember to include a selection of soft drinks: it's an irresponsible host or hostess who encourages guests who are driving to drink.

However short and informal the gathering, it really is worth taking the trouble to prepare some interesting food – bowls of crisps and peanuts just don't have the same appeal. If you invite more than fifteen people, you'll need help – glasses must be kept topped up and the food circulating. You don't want to find when they've all gone that you were so busy working you didn't have a chance to talk to any of your friends.

Left *A selection of hot and cold canapés: Brie and grapes on sticks; smoked salmon and dill, rolled in brown bread and sliced; smoked chicken or prawns wrapped in mange-tout; mini pizza slices; cheese and anchovy straws; mini chicken satay and Peanut sauce (page 138); smoked beef and fresh figs; Sesame balls (page 88).*

FINGER FOOD

Cold
◆ Chopped egg in dill mayonnaise on croûtons

◆ Sliced kiwi fruit wrapped in Parma ham

◆ Cherry tomatoes stuffed with feta or boursin cheese

◆ Chorizo and cream cheese on pumpernickel

Hot
◆ Scrambled egg on smoked salmon on rye

◆ Crab and ginger samosas

◆ Salami and Mozzarella, grilled on circles of toast

◆ Field mushrooms stuffed with pistachio nuts and freshly grated Parmesan

WINES AND COCKTAILS

Choose wines for a drinks party carefully – avoid anything too sweet, heavy or full-bodied, although on cold winter nights a cup of MULLED WINE is a lovely way to greet people.

Fine sparkling white or rosé wines or a WINE CUP, are ideal for serving with savoury canapés and crudités. Dry or medium dry white wines, such as Riesling, Muscadet or Soave, are also good or a light-bodied red wine, such as a Beaujolais, Valpolicella or Bardolino.

It's fun to experiment with cocktails too, but remember that spirit-based cocktails with several ingredients can be very expensive if you're making large quantities. It's best to leave the more exotic cocktails with furled

umbrellas to the real professionals. For the cocktails listed here, you don't need a proper cocktail shaker – mix them in a large jug, or in the glasses, using a cocktail stirrer.
◆ **Kir** or *vin blanc cassis*: white wine and crème de cassis. Put $\frac{1}{2}$ teaspoon cassis into each glass and fill with chilled wine. For a Kir Impériale put $\frac{1}{2}$ teaspoon

framboise (raspberry syrup) in a glass and fill with champagne

◆ **Bellini:** fresh peach juice in champagne

◆ **Harvey Wallbanger:** 1 measure vodka, 1 tablespoon Galliano liqueur, orange juice and ice

◆ **Pink gin:** 1 measure gin, $\frac{1}{2}$

teaspoon Angostura bitters, soda water and ice. For the non-alcoholic version, omit the gin!

◆ **Snowball:** a popular Christmas cocktail (but considered too sweet by some): 1 measure advocaat, 1 teaspoon caster sugar, beaten egg white, lemonade and dash of lime

Non-alcoholic cocktails
◆ **St Clements:** half orange juice, half bitter lemon

◆ **Parson's Walk:** half orange juice, half ginger ale, slice of orange and ice

◆ **Sportsman:** 1 measure lime cordial, 1 teaspoon Grenadine, tonic, slice of lemon and ice

BRUNCH

I never feel like breakfast first thing in the morning, but am usually too hungry to last out till lunch, so for me late morning is a very civilized time to eat. Giving a brunch can be a lovely, casual way of feeding friends too. Perhaps you have guests staying, and decide to ask a few more to join you mid-morning, or perhaps you want to entertain some friends but need to be free by the afternoon.

Brunch can be as simple or complicated as you choose, but the emphasis must be on informality – people won't expect to sit formally round a table. Make the room warm and inviting, with as many armchairs as you can muster for people to sprawl in after they've eaten, maybe even leaving a selection of newspapers lying around, particularly if it's Sunday. If you've made everyone extremely comfortable but you don't want them to stay all day, you may have to think of ways of gently persuading them to go – always a test of your social skills!

There are plenty of alternatives for food but keep it simple. I went to one brunch where Eggs Benedict was served: quite delicious, of course, but the host was so panicky about his hollandaise spoiling and his eggs going hard that I'm not sure he enjoyed a minute of it. If you do plan to offer food that has to be cooked just before serving, make sure you have some willing helpers and take turns in the kitchen.

Right *Serving a late brunch gives you the time and opportunity to cook a variety of dishes for your guests. Include both savoury and sweet things in the menu and have enough food to allow your guests second helpings. Clockwise from the left: Blueberry muffins (page 134) and a selection of hot bread rolls; scrambled eggs made with chopped bacon and mushrooms, sprinkled with chopped chives; Tuna fish cakes (page 100); Devils on horseback (prunes wrapped in bacon and baked in the oven for 15 minutes at 400°F, 200°C, gas mark 6); and an exotic fruit salad of kiwi fruit, mangoes and lychees, tossed in their own juices.*

FILLED CROISSANTS

Make a thick béchamel sauce and use it as a base for a variety of fillings.

◆ Prawns in tomato mayonnaise

◆ Pressed garlic, chopped parsley and cooked sliced mushrooms

◆ Grated cheese and chopped smoked chicken

Halve each croissant, fill and warm through in the oven.

CROQUES

Croque monsieur – a hot, fried cheese and ham sandwich – is especially popular in France. To cook, trim off the crusts, press the sandwich firmly together and fry in hot fat until browned on both sides. Drain on kitchen paper and serve. A *croque enfant* is a smaller version, cut into quarters. Arrange the fried quarters on skewers and place whole olives between them. Try adding either mayonnaise and sweet gherkin or French mustard to the filling.

OMELETTE FILLINGS

◆ Chopped cooked spinach and ricotta

◆ Fried bacon and mushrooms

◆ Chopped ham and Gruyère

◆ Diced cooked potato, peas and spring onion

◆ Sliced cooked mushroom and almonds

◆ Chopped fresh herbs (tarragon, chervil, chives) mixed into the beaten egg before cooking

If you prepare the fillings in advance and store them in the fridge, take them out an hour or so before making the omelettes so that they are not too cold.

DRINKS FOR BRUNCH

Start with a classic cocktail such as Buck's Fizz – champagne (or sparkling white wine) with orange juice – or champagne with peach, mango or apple juice. Another popular morning drink is a Bloody Mary (vodka and tomato juice) with plenty of lemon juice and Worcester sauce. For special occasions, have a few bottles of pink champagne.

If you need a good reviver cocktail at the end of a brunch party, try a measure of brandy to a measure of white crème de menthe – shaken not stirred!

For those who don't want alcohol, provide a range of fruit juices – orange, tomato, grapefruit or passion fruit – served with or without mineral water.

This has become our favourite way of entertaining. Once you have children, it's almost impossible to give a formal lunch party unless you banish them from the house. It's much more fun to let them join in, and if you invite friends with children they will have company too. People tend to be more relaxed at the weekends, and it's a good chance to gather and exchange news.

I am a bit of a traditionalist and tend to go for a roast, but it's by no means necessary. It would be much simpler to choose something that can be prepared ahead and either reheated quickly or successfully kept warm, especially if you want to be out of doors before lunch. How lovely to stroll back to the house and be greeted by the delicious smell of lunch cooking – and so much nicer if the cook is able to go along too.

If you decide to have a roast, then make the vegetables simple by braising or puréeing them. And don't forget your joint will be much easier to carve if you let it rest out of the oven for 15–20 minutes, preferably in a warm place, loosely covered with foil. This gives you time for those last-minute preparations: making the gravy, warming plates and browning roast potatoes in a hot oven. Finish off with a pudding such as trifle, crumble *(page 133)* or our rich Banana cake *(page 135)* and spend the rest of the afternoon relaxing and digesting the meal.

MEAT GLAZES

Mix to a paste and spread over the fat before roasting.

◆ **Lamb:** 1 tablespoon mint sauce to 2 brown sugar and 2 mustard

◆ **Chicken:** 30 g (1 oz) melted butter, juice and rind of 1 orange and 2 tablespoons blackcurrant jelly

◆ **Beef:** 1 tablespoon lemon juice to 2 tomato purée and 1 fresh chopped herbs

Left Clockwise from the left: *Seafood lasagne (page 105); Leek and potato purée (page 126) served with chicken drumsticks; roast lamb with Apricot sauce (page 139); Lamb korma (page 117) with boiled rice, accompanied by papadums and a selection of fruit chutneys.*

TRIFLE

This traditional English pudding, with layers of sherry-soaked sponge, jam or jelly, fruit (strawberries, raspberries or peaches are lovely), custard and cream, looks pretty served in individual glasses so that you can see the layers. For a more sophisticated version, try chocolate cake and Curaçao in place of the sponge and sherry and chocolate sauce instead of custard.

TRADITIONAL LUNCH

Roast lamb
Apricot sauce
(page 139)
Roast potatoes
Broccoli purée
(page 126)
◆
Plum crumble and
Crème Anglaise
(page 133)

LUNCH IN 60 MINUTES

Chicken drumsticks
Leek and potato purée
(page 126)
Garden peas
◆
Trifle *(left)*

LUNCH PREPARED IN ADVANCE

Seafood lasagne
(page 105)
Choice of salads
(pages 82–3)
◆
Spicy apple meringue
(page 132)

INDIAN STYLE LUNCH

Lamb korma *(page 117)*
Plain rice
Choice of salads
(pages 82–3)
◆
Exotic fruit salad
(page 38)

BARBECUES

It's so much easier to entertain outside – people can lie on the grass or in deckchairs gazing up at the sky and you won't feel you have to get them chatting, as you would indoors. There's nothing quite like the delicious smell of char-broiled sausages or kebabs wafting across the garden. Or, if you prefer, get some hickory chips and throw them onto the charcoal: they'll smell more exotic – as do dried herbs. On the subject of safety: if you're using firelighters, make sure they're the type made specifically for barbecues; *don't* use petrol.

Barbecuing may be a relaxed way of feeding your guests but it's a good idea to have a few bits and pieces to nibble while the food is cooking – it's never easy to time it exactly. Do MARINATE beforehand: it really does add enormously to both taste and texture. You might consider pre-cooking chicken on the bone and sausages for 20 minutes in a hot oven as they can easily be undercooked on the barbecue; this also reduces the perennial problem of the spitting sausage.

You'll need a pair of very long tongs – hosts with burnt arms aren't going to be the life and soul of the party. Get someone to help with the cooking and serving so the food can be eaten while it's hot. Serve it on strong, laminated paper plates: washing up would be far too prosaic and it's easier on your crockery too!

COOKING TIMES

Light the charcoal 50 minutes ahead. It always takes longer than you think to come to the perfect temperature: when the flames have died down and the charcoal is a smouldering reddish-black you can start cooking. Turn the food once during cooking and brush on extra marinade sparingly to prevent it drying out.

10 mins: steaks and hamburgers
10–15 mins: fish (slashed diagonally)
15–20 mins: sausages, lamb chops or cutlets, meat kebabs, corn on the cob (soak 1 hour in water first)
25–30 mins: pork chops or cutlets, poultry
45–50 mins: potatoes (in foil at edge of barbecue)

FOOD TO BARBECUE

Almost all lean cuts of meat barbecue well. As well as kebabs, chops, sausages and so on, try prawns marinated in Satay marinade *(page 138)*, or Tandoori chicken drumsticks *(page 111)*. Fish tends to disintegrate when cooked, so, unless you have special holders, wrap it in foil. Vegetables and fruit can be threaded onto a skewer, but choose those with a low water content.

Right *Meat kebabs; trout in fish holders; vegetable kebabs (baby sweetcorn, courgettes, carrots, peppers, onions); fruit kebabs (grapes, peaches, kiwi fruit, strawberries, bananas); bowls of Peanut and Barbecue sauce (page 138); green salad and a Wine cup (page 62).*

POTATO FACES

Let the children help here: it's great fun making BAKED POTATO faces. Provide an assortment of features (peas for teeth, salami for tongues, pineapple chunks for ears) and cocktail sticks to secure them. Perhaps it would be safest to cut mouth and eye shapes yourself.

HERB BUTTERS

Blend 120 g (4 oz) butter with any of the following.

◆ **Parsley** (with fish): 1 tablespoon lemon juice, 4 tablespoons fresh chopped parsley, salt and pepper

◆ **Basil** (with chicken or vegetables): 1 tablespoon lemon juice, 2 tablespoons fresh chopped basil, salt and pepper

◆ **Anchovy** (with meat or vegetables): 2 tablespoons anchovy paste

◆ **Garlic** (with almost anything!): 1 clove crushed garlic, 1 tablespoon lemon juice, salt and pepper

BAKED POTATOES   **57**

PICNICS

White tablecloths fluttering gently in the breeze, champagne cooling in silver buckets, fine bone china and Waterford glasses gently clinking, and four-course meals laid out by liveried footmen. Not a very attainable ideal nowadays, but a picnic is still a delightful way of entertaining either formally or informally, or of just giving the family a special day out. Like barbecues, you have to worry far less about keeping everyone happy: they will probably be very content to enjoy their surroundings. Choose your site beforehand; a string of guests wandering across the fields while you search for the perfect place can take the edge off the occasion, and the last thing you want is to have to begin negotiating with an angry bull in the middle of pudding.

Try to use pretty paper plates and attractive containers or serving dishes to decant into – some plastic tubs can be very unappealing. Plan your packing very carefully, and stack only if you are sure the interlayers are strong enough: sandwiches squashed to look like oozing pancakes would be an unattractive surprise when you arrive. Dips travel well in screw-top jars, and CRUDITÉS to accompany them could be wrapped in foil. Individual meals like our little bucket feasts are perfect for children, who can wander off and eat them in gangs away from the adults, if they want their own private picnic.

PACKING FOR PICNICS

Packing food for a picnic can be tricky, but you don't have to take the full Victorian hamper to ensure everything travels safely and in some style. If you have Chinese steamers (and they're very inexpensive), use them for plates, small bowls and cutlery, or for layers of food. A large pie or flan can be safely carried between two cake racks tied together with string; small corks placed at each corner help to keep the racks in position. Wrap glasses in napkins which have been folded into triangles and place them at the top of your basket. It's worth investing in an insulated cooler to carry drinks and anything else that needs to be kept cool.

CRUDITÉS   **15**

Left *Individual picnic buckets are great fun for children – fill them with a selection of stuffed Pitta bread (pages 46, 111 and 117), fruit juices, flapjacks, crisps and fruit.*

DON'T FORGET

◆ Corkscrew
◆ Bottle/can opener
◆ Sharp knife
◆ Napkins/paper towels/ wet wipes
◆ Bag for rubbish
◆ Insect repellent/sting cream/sun cream
◆ Something to sit on
◆ Games for children (ball or frisbee)
◆ Windbreak, sunshade (or umbrella!)

Add your own necessities – only *you* know which one-eyed teddy or intergalactic spaceship is crucial to the peace of the afternoon.

PICNIC FINGER FOOD

Dips and vegetable purées *(pages 15 and 126)*

◆

Stuffed pitta *(page 46)*
or
Quiche
Tandoori chicken drumsticks *(page 111)*

◆

Hazelnut shortbread *(page 135)*
Banana cake with peaches and pears *(page 135)*

Above *A large basket will hold all your picnic cutlery, crockery and food, but be sure to pack carefully, wrapping glasses, bottles and other breakables in thick napkins. A Tricolour fish mousse (page 99) can be safely transported in the mould and then turned out onto a plate when you arrive.*

Don't spurn sandwiches and rolls, but be adventurous with the fillings. If it's quite a large party, it's fun to label rolls, especially if guests can't eat certain foods. A hot soup taken in a thermos and served in pretty paper cups makes a good starter, or an iced one if it's a hot day. Fruit, cheese and cake are all suitable for 'afters', as long as they're easy to eat in the fingers.

If you're trying to be more formal, plan a buffet-style meal to be eaten with a fork, but keep the food relatively simple. Freshness and transportability should really be the primary considerations. A real tablecloth adds a touch of elegance to a picnic, and lots of thick paper napkins are always useful.

Drink should be packed separately, and, if you're serving white wine, it must be really well chilled: make use of one of those marvellous cool boxes. For children, small cartons of fruit juice with straws are the easiest solution but mix up squash at home if you want to be more economical. Try to include some bottled water in case it's hot, thirsty weather, and allow extra (plus a bowl) for any canine friends who are going with you!

Don't forget to take plenty of plastic bags for rubbish, dirty forks and so on: you don't want to leave any traces behind – even the odd plastic bottle top can mean death for a bird or animal.

FILLINGS FOR SANDWICHES, PITTA AND LOAVES

Use the freshest ingredients for sandwiches and be generous with fillings. A real sandwich should be thick bread, crammed with layers of food. Don't forget the HERB BUTTERS too. Try some of these fillings.

◆ Slices of ham or salami, and tomato, with chopped lettuce and pickle

◆ Chopped cooked turkey, crispy cooked bacon, raw onion and lettuce with mayonnaise

◆ Bagel filled with scrambled egg and smoked salmon

◆ Pastrami on rye bread with mild mustard and celery

◆ Sliced egg, shrimps and lettuce with mayonnaise

◆ Slices of avocado and cooked chicken with TOMATO MAYONNAISE

◆ Tuna, pesto and mayonnaise

Pitta bread Try some more substantial fillings:

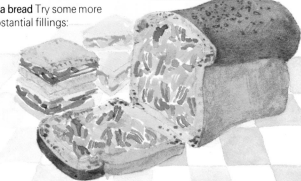

◆ Crab and raw sliced mushrooms with WALNUT AND LEMON DRESSING

◆ Cooked diced new potatoes and coriander with CURRY MAYONNAISE

◆ Fried aubergine, melted Mozzarella

◆ Curried minced beef, cucumber and coriander

Stuffed loaf Cut the top off, remove all the crumb, brush with melted butter and crisp in the oven for 10 minutes. When filled, cook in the oven at 350°F (180°C, gas mark 4) for 1 hour, wrapped in foil. Transport in the foil and serve warm or cold. Try these fillings:

◆ Chopped cooked chicken, turkey, ham or bacon with mushrooms, onions and a little stock or sherry to bind the mixture

◆ 1 tin of tuna and 1 tin of sardines combined with the juice of ½ lemon, 2 cooked mashed hard-boiled eggs and salt and pepper

Left *Super sandwiches: filled French bread and sesame seed rolls, tied with raffia to prevent the food spilling out, and labelled to identify the type of filling – cheese, sausage (or salami), fish or meat.*

Right *Sweet picnic fare that is really easy to transport – Fig fingers (page 135); Banana cake with peaches and pears (page 135); Hazelnut shortbread (page 135).*

FOOD-FILLED FRUIT AND VEGETABLES

Hollowed-out fruit and vegetables make marvellous containers for other foods – ideal for formal or informal picnics, or for buffet eating.

◆ Slice the stems off courgettes, halve them and scoop out the pulp with an apple corer. Fill with goat's cheese and pistachio nuts.

◆ Celery, chicory, and radicchio boats can be filled with a variety of SALADS.

◆ Vine or lettuce leaves, blanched spinach leaves, or cabbage leaves cooked for 2 minutes, can be wrapped around a spicy filling of cooked rice and minced meat, onions, herbs, pine nuts and seasoning, and rolled into small parcels.

◆ BAKED POTATOES, crisp or soft baked, can be hollowed out and the flesh mixed with ingredients such as cream cheese and chopped chives; tuna mayonnaise; sautéed mushrooms, pistachio nuts and chopped parsley; or shelled prawns, sour cream and lemon juice before being piled back into the skins. Transport in foil.

◆ Yellow, red and green peppers are good containers for dips, or cold ratatouille and cooked rice; add a few chopped nuts to taste.

◆ Small cherry tomatoes with the seeds and pulp removed can be filled with soft cheese, nuts and herbs, or hummus; larger tomatoes are good for ground beef and sultanas or cracked wheat and parsley.

◆ Scooped-out lemons are ideal for fish pâté; try salmon or mackerel. Replace the tops once they are filled.

◆ Fruit salad looks wonderful in a fruit case, such as a scooped-out MELON or pineapple.

◆ Scooped-out lemons and oranges can also be used for Lime and orange syllabub *(page 130)*, which needs a little gelatine to set.

◆ Remove the flesh from baked aubergines and use as stuffing with cooked tomato, garlic and almonds. Cook for 10 minutes at 350°F (180°C, gas mark 4).

LATE-NIGHT SUPPERS

It's lovely to invite people back after the theatre or some other evening outing, as long as it doesn't mean settling down to lots of late-night preparation and cooking.

The most important thing of all is to have something ready for people to nibble with their drinks while you prepare the rest of the meal: a dip, perhaps, or some king prawns with brown bread and garlic butter or mayonnaise. The main meal should consist of food that can either be reheated, served cold, or cooked very simply and quickly. You certainly won't want anything too heavy, so avoid cheese or too much cream. Perhaps an interesting soup that you can warm up, served with crusty French bread, followed by a substantial salad. Use the type of cooking pot that can transfer directly to the table, and don't plan on preparing vegetables after you get in: you won't feel like chopping and slicing. A rice dish would be another excellent solution: filling but not too solid. It's unlikely anyone will want a proper pudding, but you could put a good selection of fresh fruit on the table.

Your menu will depend on whether you have to prepare the night or morning before or have time to pop back in the early evening. Before you leave, put the wine in the fridge if it's white or open it if it's red (only if you're back in the early evening) and don't forget to take the butter and pre-cooked casserole out of the fridge.

Left *Light, easy-to-digest dishes are what's called for in late-night eating sessions. Clockwise from the left: Avocado dip (page 88) with some mixed crudités and prawns; Chicken and black olive casserole (page 109); Chicken pilau (page 112); Almond soup (page 95); Herb mayonnaise (page 82) with a selection of mixed crudités, king prawns and sliced eggs.*

LATE SUPPER PREPARED IN ADVANCE
Mushroom soup *(page 94)*
or
Almond soup *(page 95)*
◆
Chicken pilau *(page 112)*
◆
Dried fruit salad

LATE SUPPER PREPARED IN ADVANCE
Crudités *(page 15)*
Avocado dip *(page 88)*
Herb mayonnaise *(page 82)*
◆
Chicken and black olive casserole *(page 109)*
Choice of salads *(pages 82–3)*
French bread
◆
Spicy apple meringue *(page 132)*
or
Lime and orange syllabub *(page 130)*

A VERY SPECIAL TEA

Teatime: a delightful English tradition now enjoyed in many parts of the world. It's a meal that can include anything from a large plate of hot, cooked food to a few dainty cucumber sandwiches. This is the perfect time for a christening or naming celebration, for entertaining friends with children, or just for an unusual party: it's one of the easiest meals to prepare for large numbers because there's only one course and everything can be served cold – except the cup of tea itself!

If it's the birth of a child you're celebrating, it's a lovely opportunity for decorating the room, choosing a blue or pink colour scheme. Looping up the tablecloth with bows is very simple to do and looks wonderful: imagine how pretty it would be to use both pink and blue ribbon for boy and girl twins!

You'll probably want to include sandwiches but you can make them look more attractive than usual with the trick we've used here. Cake is a must for any tea party, especially a christening, and it can make a lovely centrepiece. Offer more than one kind of tea to drink – China and Indian or something more exotic – or perhaps champagne 'to wet the baby's head'. If children are among the guests and they're not too tiny, it's a good idea to put them on a separate, lower table: they'll feel grown-up and it'll give the adults more chance to talk.

GRAND SANDWICHES

Spiral sandwiches look good. Cut a loaf into slices lengthways, trim off the crusts, spread with your chosen filling, and roll up carefully to make 'Swiss rolls'. Cut each roll into 2.5 cm (1 in) thick pieces.

◆ Smoked salmon and HERB BUTTER

◆ Crab, flaked almonds and mayonnaise

◆ Cream cheese, peach and walnuts

◆ Chopped egg and asparagus tips

◆ Cooked chicken and chutney in mayonnaise with a pinch of curry powder

CHRISTENING OR NAMING CAKE

1 round fruit cake – 20 cm (8 in) deep; egg-cup; flour for dusting; 1 packet 450 g (1 lb) FONDANT ICING, (reserve small piece and colour rest blue or pink); 1 tablespoon sieved jam for sticking; 340 g (¾ lb) marzipan; 225 g (½ lb) ROYAL ICING; blue or pink ribbon, pins, small fresh flowers

Roll out a piece of white fondant icing and wrap around a floured egg-cup to

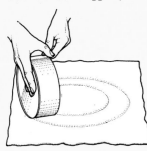

make a little vase (fit so that you can pull it off easily when dry). Leave to dry. Spread the fruit cake with jam and cover with rolled-out marzipan. Roll out the coloured fondant and make a light impression on it with a 20 cm (8 in) cake tin. Roll the side of the tin round the circle, marking an outer larger circle (see below), and cut out the larger circle. Moisten the top of the cake with water and drape the icing over it. Pipe loops of royal icing around the sides of the 'cloth', using a star nozzle. Position tiny ribbon bows at the top of the loops with pins. Unmould the vase and secure on top of the cake with royal icing. Fill with small flowers, and stick onto the cake with a little icing.

A VERY SPECIAL TEA

Triple-deckered or spiral sandwiches

◆

Filo triangles *(page 89)*

◆

Small meringues
Plain and chocolate-dipped Vienna biscuits *(page 134)*
Spiral biscuits *(pages 54 and 134)*
or
Hazelnut shortbread *(page 135)*

◆

Christening cake

Right *Triple-deckered sandwiches with a variety of fillings; chocolate-dipped Vienna biscuits; meringues; Spiral biscuits; Filo triangles.*

BIRTHDAY PARTIES

HUMPTY INVITATIONS

It's fun to make invitations to suit your party theme. Fold a piece of card in half. On one side, draw an incomplete egg shape which has a straight edge along the fold and at the bottom. Draw in Humpty's face, arms and clothes and cut him out. Make sure you don't cut along the fold or your card won't stand up.

Once you have children, tea parties become a regular part of your life. Invitations to birthdays, Christmas parties and after-school gatherings come thick and fast, and it's the best possible way of helping your child to make friends, and of getting to know some of the parents too. Birthdays are the most important, and have to be celebrated with all due ceremony.

Up to the age of five or six limit the number of guests to no more than ten or twelve. If you invite too many children they will just find it overwhelming; at this age they play far more happily with a small group of close friends. Later on, when your child is older, it's fun to have more if you can bear the chaos.

It's good to build the party around a theme, something the guest of honour is keen on at the time, as long as it's not too demanding: for his second birthday one of my children insisted on having a cake shaped like a vacuum cleaner! As they get a little older, ask the guests to come in suitable costumes. Nothing expensive: fun rather than style is the key note.

For a first and second birthday you won't need games; just playing together with toys will keep everyone happy, but from then on you should plan in advance. Have some game ready to play as soon as they arrive so that you don't have groups of little ones standing around, looking shyly at

PARTY THEMES

◆ Fairy-story characters (such as Cinderella, Beauty and the Beast or Pinocchio)

◆ Animals for a Noah's Ark or zoo party

◆ Cartoon characters (such as Mickey or Minnie Mouse or Rupert Bear)

◆ Favourite colours – with food and table decorations to match

◆ National costumes – from anywhere in the world

◆ Favourite sports

◆ Favourite characters from TV programmes

◆ Heroes and heroines – superheroes, or simply anyone they admire!

IDEAS FOR FOOD

◆ Sandwiches shaped like animals: popular fillings are cream cheese and cucumber; peanut butter; marmite; egg mayonnaise; banana and honey

◆ Carrot and celery sticks to dip into cream cheese or mayonnaise and tomato ketchup

◆ Cheese and pineapple on cocktail sticks: spear into grapefruit halves to make savoury hedgehogs

◆ Faces piped onto digestive biscuits with cream cheese: highlight eyes with raisins

◆ Crisps and some sweets: after all birthdays come only once a year – but keep till after the savouries!

HUMPTY DUMPTY CAKE

2 Madeira or loaf-tin cakes – 20 × 13 × 9 cm (8 × 5 × 3½ in); 450 g (1 lb) BUTTERCREAM; 5 × 225 g (½ lb) packets FONDANT ICING, 3 coloured brown, 1 yellow, ⅔ (150 g) red, ⅓ (75 g) white; 125 g (4 oz) white ROYAL ICING; 1 chocolate Easter egg; square or rectangular cake or bread board; 225 g (½ lb) cream cheese; 225 g (½ lb) chocolate buttercream; 120 g (4 oz) chopped nuts or crushed digestive biscuits; whole hazelnuts; raw vegetables; small sweets

The Wall
Trim the edges of the cakes and sandwich the two cakes together (one on top of the other) with buttercream. Spread a thin layer of plain buttercream over the sides and top of the wall and cover with brown fondant icing, doing one side at a time to get a good sharp edge to the wall. Dampen the surface with a little water to help the icing stick and then pipe a brick effect with white royal icing. Leave to harden.

Humpty Dumpty
Cover half the egg with yellow fondant. Roll a long band of red fondant icing and make a bow tie to wrap round the middle of the egg. Roll two 'legs' in white fondant and cover them with yellow fondant, rolling it round the legs to make trousers but leaving the feet exposed. Gently stick the legs onto the wall with a little royal icing. Press the egg gently down onto the wall so that it rests on the legs. Make 'arms' in the same way, rolling them in yellow fondant 'sleeves', and stick onto Humpty, with the hands resting on the wall. Colour a little royal icing for the eyes and mouth and pipe the features onto the egg.

The Garden
Cover half a cake board with softened cream cheese and half with chocolate buttercream. Position Humpty and wall at one end of it. Make a path down the middle of the 'garden' with chopped nuts or digestive biscuits and plant vegetable tops on the cheese side, sweets on the icing side. Mark the edge of the path with hazelnuts and sweets.

BUTTERCREAM	10
ICING	10

INITIAL BISCUITS

Cut a biscuit in the shape of the initial letter of each guest's name using the Cinnamon hearts mix *(page 134)*. Bake and ice in different colours. Or pipe initials using the Vienna biscuits recipe *(page 134)*.

Alternatively, make round, square or crescent-shapes and pipe faces onto them.

each other. A good 'ice-breaker' is to cut big colour pictures from magazines in two, give half a picture to each child and let them find the matching piece.

At this age, whoever brought them will stay, so you should have plenty of willing helpers. Lay the table early in the day so you can concentrate on the food. If possible, try to sit the children all in chairs or high chairs at a table – I've tried sitting them on the floor but far more things get spilt and it's difficult to stop them wandering off in the middle of tea and decorating your sofa with chocolatey fingers. For the last few parties I've hired low tables and chairs, but I know some mothers have managed to borrow them from their children's playschool.

Make the meal itself as healthy as possible: most children love raw fruit and vegetables – it doesn't have to be all sweet biscuits and cakes. Presentation is everything: food made into shapes, faces, animals and so on is far more likely to be eaten. And don't make the birthday cake too large, most children only want a tiny piece. Have a huge supply of wet cloths ready for accidents and sticky faces/hands, and offer bathroom visits frequently! When they're a little older, it's fun to hire an entertainer, such as a magician or a puppeteer, for a show after tea. Don't forget the now obligatory 'going-home bags', and you may want to offer your parent-helpers a drink too.

Right An animal theme for a party can be great fun to do and children love it. Make the polar bears from meringue. For 350 g (12 oz) meringue, whisk 4 egg whites until stiff, add 100 g (4 oz) caster sugar and whisk until it is smooth and stands in stiff peaks, then fold in another 100 g (4 oz) sugar. Draw a polar bear template on thick card, place baking parchment paper on top and pipe polar bear shapes until you have used up the meringue. Place on a baking tray and bake on the lowest shelf in the oven, preheated to 225°F (110°C, gas mark ¼), for 2–3 hours until firm; leave to cool.

For the fish bowl, make a lemon and lime jelly and leave to set in a glass bowl. When set, insert white chocolate fish, chocolate animals or pink prawns (bought from confectioners) in the jelly. Don't use candied sweets like jelly beans as the colour tends to 'bleed'.

HOW TO MAKE A PARTY MAYPOLE

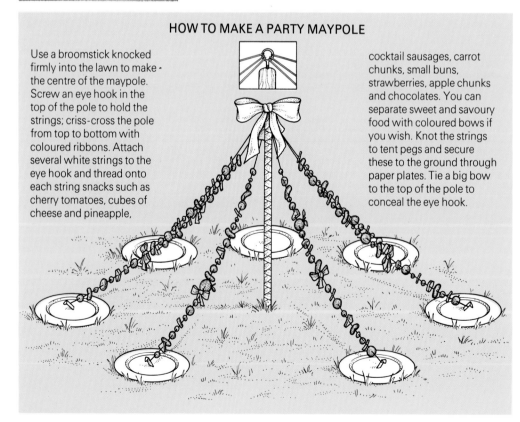

Use a broomstick knocked firmly into the lawn to make the centre of the maypole. Screw an eye hook in the top of the pole to hold the strings; criss-cross the pole from top to bottom with coloured ribbons. Attach several white strings to the eye hook and thread onto each string snacks such as cherry tomatoes, cubes of cheese and pineapple,

cocktail sausages, carrot chunks, small buns, strawberries, apple chunks and chocolates. You can separate sweet and savoury food with coloured bows if you wish. Knot the strings to tent pegs and secure these to the ground through paper plates. Tie a big bow to the top of the pole to conceal the eye hook.

SPIRAL BISCUITS

Using the Cinnamon hearts recipe *(page 134)*, divide the mixture into two batches and colour one batch with FOOD COLOURING. Roll out each batch separately and carefully lay one on top of the other. Gently roll it up like a Swiss roll. Chill in the fridge for 30 minutes and cut into 0.6 cm (¼ in) slices. Bake in the oven for 12 minutes at 325°F (160°C, gas mark 3). Leave to cool and then transfer with a spatula onto a cold surface to crisp up.

FOOD COLOURING   **10**

SNAKE CAKE

8 mini Swiss rolls; 4 × 225 g (½ lb) packets FONDANT ICING, coloured yellow; 120 g (4 oz) fondant icing, coloured red; 15 g (½ oz) fondant icing, coloured black; kitchen paper; green and brown FOOD COLOURING; 2 silver balls

Place the mini rolls end to end and roll out yellow fondant to a slightly longer length – allow an extra 10 cm (4 in) each end – and about 20 cm (8 in) in width. Trim the corners off the Swiss rolls to make coiling the snake easier. Place the rolls, curved side down, on the fondant, leaving the extra space at each end. Fold round, trimming and wetting edges to join. Trim the fondant diagonally at one end to make a pointed tail and reserve all the trimmings. Shape the other end to make the lower jaw. Make the upper jaw and head from the yellow trimmings and attach to the lower jaw, smoothing the join firmly with wet fingers. Roll out enough red fondant to make the mouth and tongue. Stick the mouth to the lower and upper jaw with moistened fondant and prop open with crumpled kitchen paper. Carefully coil the snake and paint a pattern on the 'skin' using the food colouring. When the fondant is dry, remove the paper from the mouth and stick the tongue in place with moistened fondant. Make two eyes from black fondant, moisten and attach to the head. Add silver balls for pupils.

IDEAS FOR FOOD

◆ Grown-up sandwich fillings like avocado and bacon, tuna or chopped egg with CURRIED MAYONNAISE

◆ Mini pizzas

◆ Hamburgers and cheeseburgers with mild relishes and ketchup

◆ Slices of giant watermelon

◆ Fresh fruit on long wooden skewers: grapes, tangerines and apple pieces are good. (Add soft-centred chocolates and it's a hit!)

◆ Popcorn lucky dip

◆ Cola and lemonade (usual prohibitions are lifted for birthday treats!)

As children grow older, birthday parties become even more important: for a seven-year-old it can be the focus of the social year! Themes remain extremely popular. A favourite book, film, television character or subject at school may give you a clue, but there are several that seem to survive the generation gaps: dinosaurs, fairies, circuses, jungles, ballerinas, knights, pirates, and so on. When my daughter was seven, she wanted all her friends to dress up as princesses, but one of them refused to come as something so 'old fashioned'. We had to write 'princesses or punks' on the invitations instead: it was certainly a very interesting mixture.

As the children will be dropped off and left on their own, you may need to enlist a couple of helpers: it's essential that things are kept reasonably under control or a party can disintegrate into feuding groups. Plan some interesting games – those involving teams work well at this age when the competitive spirit is really developing. After tea, if you can run to the expense, a professional entertainer is still much enjoyed, and it gives a peaceful hour or so for you to relax and enjoy the afternoon yourself.

Serve lots of savoury things for tea: tastes are becoming more sophisticated. However, ice-cream still goes down very well, and the home-made kind is fairly simple to make, following your theme if possible.

FAVOURITE GAMES

◆ **Hat parade** Each guest makes a hat from coloured papers, stickers, glitter, ribbon and glue; the best hat wins

◆ **Drawing race** Form two teams and give a member of each a paper slip bearing identical subjects, like 'the first man to watch TV' or 'the heel on Cinderella's glass slipper'. Both team members return to their teams and draw the subject. The teams must guess the exact words on the slip and the drawer may answer only 'yes' or 'no' to questions asked. As soon as the subject is guessed, the next team member goes for another subject and so on. The first team to guess all the subjects wins.

DOUBLOON CAKE

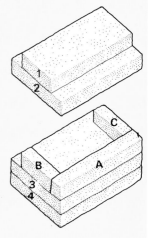

and sandwich on slab 2. Cover 'lid' and 'base' with chocolate ice-cream and freeze. When hardened, fill base with coins and sweets and prop lid on top. Decorate with bands of liquorice and place on a sugared cake board.

2 × 20 × 30cm (18 × 12 in) sponge cakes; 2 tablespoons jam; 1 small tub vanilla ice-cream; 1 large tub chocolate ice-cream; chocolate coins; assorted sweets; 2 liquorice whirls; rectangular board; 120 g (4 oz) brown sugar

Cut cakes crossways to make 4 slabs. Spread slab 4 with jam and vanilla ice-cream and sandwich with slab 3. Cut slab 1 as shown and stick pieces A, B and C onto slab 3 with jam. Spread one side of remainder of slab 1 with jam

FROSTING GLASSES

It's simple to add a little sophistication by serving drinks in frosted glasses. Put very lightly beaten egg white in one saucer and sifted caster sugar in another. Dip the rim of each glass into egg and then sugar. Leave to dry for 30 minutes. Or, instead of using egg white, rub the rims with lemon before dipping into sugar.

Musical bumps and rabbits popping out of hats are not going to keep a group of twelve-year-olds happy. Birthday parties have to become far more adult and sophisticated occasions. What about hiring a disco? Or it may be that an outing to a film, play or exhibition with a few very close friends would be more appreciated. Taking a group swimming or hiring a video-tape to be watched at home are other possibilities.

However you decide to entertain them, they will have to be fed, and something like our 'spud bar' with a choice of different toppings is ideal – and not too expensive. It's also very practical to come back to if you've all been on an outing. You could do something similar with PIZZAS: setting out plain bases and letting them assemble their own toppings before cooking them. You can make the drinks a little more exciting too, as a change from the usual fizzy drinks. 'Cocktails' are fun and look very special if you frost the glasses.

Ice-cream – buy one of the wholesome types – is probably the best follow-up for baked potatoes. Pile it up into a pyramid and stick candles or sparklers on top if it's replacing the traditional birthday cake: it's worth investing in a proper scoop if you haven't got one. Serve a selection of toppings and sauces to make it special and again let the children help themselves.

BAKING POTATOES

Large potatoes need to bake for at least 1 hour at 200°C (400°F, gas mark 6), but will cook faster on a metal skewer. Prick the skins before cooking to prevent them bursting. To crisp the skins, brush with butter and sprinkle with salt; for soft ones, bake in foil.

Below *A spud bar with a selection of fillings for baked potatoes is fun for hungry children. Clockwise from the left: prawn mayonnaise; carrot, apple and raisins; grated cheese; baked beans with crispy bacon; chilli con carne; and sweetcorn with chopped peppers. You can make coloured 'cocktails' in frosted cocktail glasses by adding a dash of crème de menthe or cassis to lemonade, or grenadine to orange juice. Serve milk shakes too.*

MIDSUMMER

There's something magical about eating out of doors. Whether it's in a large garden or on a tiny balcony, this is a wonderful way to enjoy the long, warm summer evenings. Outdoor entertaining is far easier – people feel relaxed away from the formality of a dining room, and in summer there's plenty of delicious and attractive food from which to choose.

Your setting can be as formal or informal as you like, but make sure you have arranged some lighting for after dusk – our simple bag lights are lovely – otherwise it can become very gloomy. Don't forget safety when planning your lighting. If you're going to eat outside regularly, it's worth getting a professional electrician to set up some garden lighting – even if you supplement it with more romantic candlelight. On hot summer nights set up some insect-repellent burners or joss sticks, as the gnats and mosquitoes may also be looking for a meal. If you don't have a garden overflowing with exotic or unusual flowers, don't worry . . . even the humble cabbage can become a glorious centrepiece with a little help.

Right *A dream supper beneath the trees, with Chinese lanterns hung from branches and bag lights casting a glow in the dusk. The table is set* *for food, while to the extreme right wine and glasses are chilled in a charming Victorian washstand filled with crushed ice.*

MAKING BAG LAMPS

Safe, very pretty lights can be made by putting candles into greaseproof paper bags. Fill a bag, white or coloured, one third full of sand. Put enough sand into a jam jar to hold a candle upright, and bury the jar in the bag of sand. Light the candle and a soft glow will illuminate the bag. Place the lights around the garden for outdoor buffets.

ICE FLOWER BOWLS

You can keep summer drinks cool very simply in a bowl of ice. Place your drinks bowl inside a larger one and cram as much crushed ice as possible between the two. The plainer the bowls the better as you can decorate the ice with borage or mint leaves or tiny summer flowers. Fill the inner bowl with a WHITE WINE CUP or Pimms.

WHITE WINE CUP   62

You're likely to feel warmer than your guests if you've been cooking and rushing about, so remember that the temperature outside can drop suddenly as it gets dark — it might be worth having sweaters on hand to offer to the chilly — and if it gets really cold you may need to move inside. In any case you must bear in mind the unpleasant possibility that it might rain. Make some contingency plans: you must be able to move into the house without too much of an upheaval.

The food itself should be easily transportable and not dependent on split-second timing: a soufflé that has to be rushed straight from oven to table and eaten immediately is obviously not going to be a very practical choice, for instance. Cold food is probably best and needn't be boring. Make your midsummer theme always one of coolness, crispness and freshness.

Left *Beautifully simple summer centrepieces for indoors or out — an arrangement of garden flowers and leaves in a shallow dish of water; lettuce leaves and camomile in an earthenware pot; cabbage leaves interspersed with pink begonia in a copper saucepan.*

Right *Table set for a midsummer evening meal – Chicken in walnut sauce (page 109); Bulgar wheat salad (page 127); salad of lettuce leaves and edible nasturtium flowers in a vinaigrette dressing. A few home-made bag lights (page 58) provide the finishing touch.*

HOW TO PREPARE MEAT TO SERVE COLD

◆ **Roast beef** Prepare your rib roast or sirloin this way and it will be rare inside, well roasted on the outside.

Ask your butcher to chine the meat, if necessary. Heat the oven to 500°F (250°C, gas mark 10). Put the meat, fat side up, on a rack over a roasting tin. Rub 1 tablespoon olive oil, salt and black pepper into the fat (you can also insert slivers of garlic). Cook the beef in the oven for 5 minutes per pound. Switch off the oven and leave the meat for 2 hours: make sure you don't open the oven door.

◆ **Chicken** Make a bouillon for the chicken with 1 onion, 2 carrots, salt and pepper. Place the chicken in a pan just large enough to take it and cover with the cold bouillon. Bring to a boil and simmer gently for 45 minutes. Leave the chicken in the bouillon until it is completely cold.

MELON SALAD

Melon looks wonderful filled with fruit salad. If the skin is dark green, it can be decorated by scoring a simple pattern with a potato peeler: a sort of fruity lino-cut. Score a line around the top of the melon and cut off the 'lid'. Hollow out and fill with a mixture of fruit, including the melon. Reposition the lid on top.

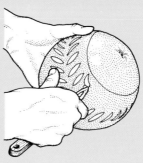

Right *Serve cold desserts for an al fresco summer meal – they can be made in advance and stored in the fridge. Lemon soufflé (page 129) with crystallized rose petals (page 11); Quick fruit tart (page 132) with seasonal fruit – star fruit, kumquats, black grapes and kiwi fruit – arranged in a decorative pattern. Try to choose fruits that look pretty together. Nightlights floating in a bowl of water add to the romance of eating outdoors.*

SUMMER SUPPER

Iced avocado soup
(page 94)

◆

Beef, potato and olive
salad *(page 115)*
Choice of salads
(pages 82–3)

◆

Quick fruit tart
(page 132)

DRINKS FOR SUMMER PARTIES

Decorate refreshing wine cups with sprigs of lemon balm or mint and slices of fresh fruit, and keep chilled. Sparkling wine or champagne looks and tastes delicious with fresh strawberries or raspberries floating on top; home-made ginger beer or lemonade, or Pimms with cucumber slices and mint, can be served from large glass jugs. Mix summer cocktails in individual glasses.

◆ **White wine cup** (makes 12 glasses): 2 bottles dry white wine, 1 bottle lemonade, slices of orange and lemon, sprigs of mint

◆ **Mint julep** (per glass): 1 measure bourbon, 1 teaspoon caster sugar, sprig of mint to decorate

◆ **Sangria** (makes 12 glasses): infuse summer fruits in 2 bottles red wine and 1 measure brandy, 85 g (3 oz) sugar and ice for at least 30 minutes. Serve with or without fruit

◆ **Milk shakes** (per glass): put chilled milk and the fruit of your choice – mango, banana, raspberry or strawberry – in a liquidizer and blend until smooth. Top with slices of fruit.

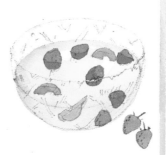

SUMMER SUPPER

Spinach mousse
(page 91)
Avocado and
Mozzarella salad
(page 81)

◆

Chicken in walnut
sauce *(page 109)*
Bulgar wheat salad
(page 127)
Flower salad *(page 60)*

◆

Lemon soufflé with
crystallized rose petals
(pages 11 and 129)

My children love celebrating Hallowe'en and we usually invite some of their friends round for a party. I take a little time making the house look as spooky as possible, but, if there are very young children around, resist making it too frightening. We play all the traditional games — buns on strings, bobbing apples and so on. But their favourite is when I dress up as a witch and we all sit in the dark while I tell the story of eating a juicy little boy. As I am talking, I pass round 'bits of him' for them to feel: peeled grapes for eyes, cooked spaghetti for veins, chicken skin for his skin, and so on! Very gruesome, but they love it.

It's lovely to be able to move outdoors for this sort of party — and for bonfire night it is essential. All our food can be carried outside: soup in a thermos or tin mugs and filled pitta bread wrapped in napkins. Sausages are always popular and so are BAKED POTATOES pre-cooked, wrapped in foil, and placed in the embers. Everything would work equally well indoors if it rained. For a special treat serve a delicious MULLED WINE and a warm, NON-ALCOHOLIC PUNCH for the children.

If it's bonfire night, you'll need fireworks — but do give responsible adults the job of guarding them and setting them off. Don't let children go anywhere near them, and, if you think your garden might be too small for safety, don't risk it: just stick to sparklers.

CARRIER BAG LIGHT

A carrier bag light is an easy special effect to make for a Hallowe'en party. Take a plain brown paper carrier bag and, on one side, cut out a face (the more frightening the better!). Half fill a jam jar with sand and insert a candle or night-light. When lit, the face will glow eerily in the dark.

HOT FOOD
TO EAT OUTSIDE

Tomato soup (*page 75*)

◆

Lamb pitta (*page 117*)
or
Chicken pitta (*page 111*)
Sausages
Meat kebabs
(*pages 42 and 138*)
Baked potatoes
(*pages 47 and 57*)

◆

Toffee-apple witches
Pumpkin pie (*page 133*)

Left *A hollowed-out pumpkin with gruesome features, tin mugs with grotesque motifs made from sticky-backed plastic, and black and orange tissue paper decorations, all help to create the right atmosphere for a Hallowe'en feast.*

HOW TO MAKE A GHOST

Your party can be really spooky with a floating ghost. Blow up a round balloon and attach a piece of string to its top knot. Thread the other end of the string through the middle of an old white sheet and tie it to a hook in the ceiling. Cut two staring eye shapes from sticky-backed black plastic tape, or some luminous material, and stick them onto the sheet as shown.

HARVEST AND THANKSGIVING

Autumn – or fall – can be the best season of the year. Its characteristic 'mists and mellow fruitfulness' are lovely and its sunshine is somehow very precious. Whether you are celebrating Harvest Festival or Thanksgiving, there are many wonderful meals you can prepare from autumnal ingredients, and the possibilities for decoration are endless. Symbols of fertility and plenty, such as corn dollies or wheatsheaves, are appropriate, and our flour-paste napkin rings and place markers will complement your table beautifully. The vine leaves and grapes we show clustered on the curtain tie-backs give a marvellous sense of nature coming to fruition too.

As you may well have people staying with you, it's important to prepare as much as possible in advance. The traditional choice for Thanksgiving is still TURKEY but our menus offer a couple of good alternatives, or you could use these recipes for another family meal over the holiday period. The chicken in a pumpkin not only looks marvellous but is very simple to cook. Raised pies should really be made as their name implies: raising the pastry by hand from a shapeless lump to form the traditional oval. I find this extremely tricky and it's far easier to use a tin. Decorate the top of the pie with pastry leaves, acorns or wheatsheaves; I sometimes paint the decoration with food colouring too.

PASTRY SHEAVES AND NAPKIN RINGS

A pastry wheatsheaf makes a lovely seasonal table decoration. Using a FLOUR AND WATER PASTE, roll out about 14 thin 'straws'. Reserve 3 or 4 for the tie, and flatten each of the remainder at one end, marking the corn 'ears' with a blunt knife. Gather the straws into a sheaf, arranging the stems side by side, and bind with the ties. Bake in a low oven until lightly browned – about 10 minutes.

To make a napkin ring, roll out two thicker straws. Twist one round the other and join the resulting 'plait'. Don't try eating either!

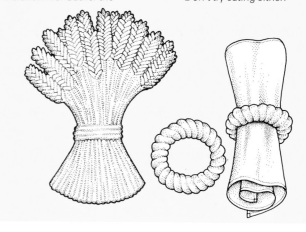

LEAFY TIE-BACKS

This wonderfully autumnal curtain tie-back is very simple to make. Taking a length of strong tape, make a loop at either end. Attach plastic vine leaves and grapes (you can buy very convincing ones now) with wire to half the binding. Making sure the decorated half of the tape faces into the room, wrap the binding round the curtain to contain it and fasten both loops to a nail on the wall behind.

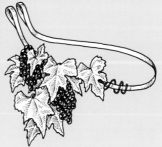

Right *Chicken in a pumpkin (page 110) is a spectacular dish to put in the centre of the table for a celebratory Thanksgiving or Harvest meal. Cooking the chicken inside the pumpkin keeps it tender.*

HARVEST THANKSGIVING SUPPER

Pumpkin soup *(page 94)*

◆

Chicken in a pumpkin *(page 110)*
Leek and tomato purée *(page 126)*

◆

Quick fruit tart *(page 132)*
or
Banana cake with peaches and pears *(page 135)*

Above From the left: *some delicious cold autumnal or fall fare: Raised game pie (page 112); White wine cup (page 62); pastry basket and bowl with seasonal fruit; Spiced plums (page 139).*

HARVEST THANKSGIVING SUPPER

Mushroom soup
(page 94)
Garlic bread

◆

Raised game pie
(page 112)
Spiced plums *(page 139)*
Two-tone cabbage
(page 124)

◆

Stuffed pears with
chocolate sauce
(page 132)

CHRISTMAS

The secret of enjoying Christmas is to plan ahead very thoroughly, get as much as possible done before the great day, then relax and not worry about what you haven't managed to do. Start early by making lists. Write down everything you think you've got to do and then try to cross off at least a quarter of them. Ditch anything irrelevant or unnecessary and delegate wherever you can.

Begin by accumulating presents whenever you see something you know would be liked, and if you're going to send Christmas cards, get them out of the way quickly. I take mine to rehearsals and write them during my scenes off. When buying cards, wrapping paper and presents, help a good cause by making use of the charity catalogues that flood through the letter-box: mail order is particularly useful when you've so much else to do.

Decorating the house is always enormous fun. We have a collection of paper and tinsel decorations that gets dragged out every year; from time to time I prune it a bit and buy a few new ones. We like a real tree, and cover it with all sorts of bits and pieces that we've collected over the years. Remember to keep your tree watered so that it doesn't shed its needles so much, or you can spray the tree with fixative, and there are fake trees that look wonderful too – I'm all for cheating in whatever possible way seems to make it easier to cope.

Right *Not everyone has a festive fire blazing in the grate, but you can warm the hearth with orange and red flowers and berries, lit from behind. Clip some candles to a bed of fir branches and cones on the mantelpiece. Add laurel leaves and mimosa – the smell of the little yellow flowers is intoxicating. When friends arrive for drinks, it's fun to serve mulled wine with mince pies and filo crackers (above), instead of filo triangles. They are surprisingly easy to make (page 89); twist the ends of the crackers, pinch hard and bake. Add the ribbon before serving.*

Make a centrepiece for the table, however simple: if there are children around, they'd probably love to help you. Take a little time to decorate the food – again children can be enthusiastic and willing helpers: cutting pastry holly-leaves for the mince pies and so on. Where food is concerned there are all sorts of crafty ways to cut corners. However much you decide to cheat, don't feel guilty about it. Depending on how much time I have, some years I make everything from scratch, and other years buy much of it ready-made. If you have a microwave, this is when it really comes into its own. Christmas pudding cooks beautifully in just 4 minutes, instead of several hours steaming away on top of your cooker.

If it's to be a family gathering, ask some of them to help – they may be only too pleased to be given a task. My sister's mother-in-law makes marvellous mince pies, for instance; my mother brings her wickedly lethal brandy butter; my aunt does the bread sauce, and so on. Make sure everyone tells them how wonderful it is and they'll do it year after year – eventually I shall end up with nothing to do!

Finally, enjoy it! I resolved long ago not to let it get on top of me, and to enjoy my children and the day as much as possible, without feeling harassed. It matters much more to everyone that you're relaxed and in a good mood rather than that every last detail is perfect.

CHRISTMAS CENTREPIECE

Tapers make lovely table decorations and they don't block everyone's view as much as candles. Take some petits-fours cases (small, shaped moulds) and half fill each one with plasticine. Cover the plasticine with rose hips, or any other winter berries, and stick a taper into each case. Arrange the cases on a large plate covered with a gold doily and light the tapers.

GIFT WRAPS

◆ Home-made sweets in cellophane, tied with ribbon and tinsel

◆ Very special chocolates in silver bags, tied with chocolate-brown ribbon

◆ Small soaps in gold or silver net, tied with matching ribbon

◆ Tiny presents hidden in children's slippers

◆ Presents wrapped in plain white paper, decorated with white paper fans: add gold glitter if you wish

◆ Plain-wrapped parcels, decorated with cut-out pictures from old Christmas cards and tied with coloured ribbon. Add a few stick-on gold or silver stars

HOW TO MAKE CHRISTMAS GARLANDS

A Christmas garland hung on your front door is a lovely way to welcome guests – and you can easily make your own. The simplest decoration is a bunch of laurel or bay tied with tinsel. For a garland frame, you need a roll of fine chicken wire. Cover with evergreen foliage and add pine or spruce cones, ribbon, glass balls, or red berries cupped in doilies.

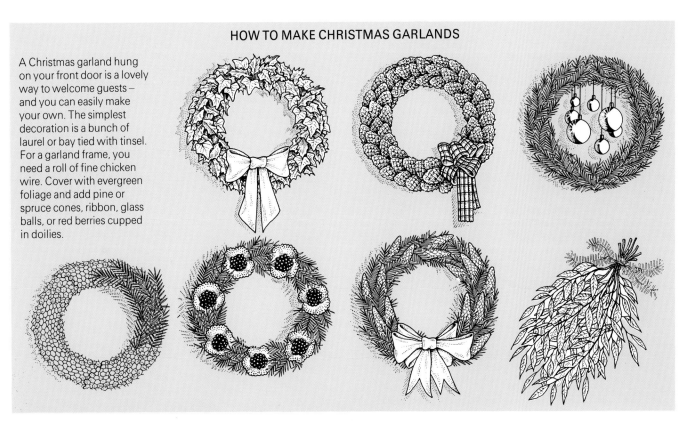

Left *Another simple but effective Christmas decoration, or table centrepiece, is a collection of gold (or silver) fruit candles. Use some fresh fruit – apples, oranges, tangerines and grapes are ideal – mixed with wax fruit candles. Make a hole in the real fruit with an apple corer, pour wax into it and insert a wick (see page 23 for instructions). Paint the fruit gold or silver with food colouring and leave to dry. Cored apples can be used as candle holders.*

Opposite above *If you are lucky enough to have a pair of bay trees, they look lovely dressed for Christmas with red and white flowers, berries and ribbon.*

Left *Make individual Christmas puddings in ramekin dishes or dariole moulds. These cook much more quickly than a large pudding – in about 30 minutes. When serving, decorate them with whipped cream and top with holly pastry-leaves painted with food colouring.*

Right *A vegetarian meal for Christmas or a special dinner party. Clockwise from the left: Roquefort roulade (page 105) with a julienne of vegetables; Tomato and basil sorbet (page 90); Spinach mousse (page 91).*

CHRISTMAS HOLIDAY DINNER

Filo crackers *(page 89)*

◆

Glazed ham *(page 119)*
Spiced plums *(page 139)*
Herbed garlic potatoes
(page 123)
Glazed carrots
Brussels sprouts

◆

Individual Christmas
puddings
Ice-cream

CELEBRATORY VEGETARIAN DINNER

Spinach mousse
(page 91)
or
Almond soup *(page 95)*

◆

Tomato and basil
sorbet *(page 90)*

◆

Roquefort roulade
(page 105)
Julienne of vegetables

◆

Mince pies

HOW TO IMPROVE THE CHRISTMAS MEAL

◆ **Starter** Consommé is traditional, but many prefer a lighter appetizer – melon with avocado in a mint dressing, or even grilled grapefruit. Consommé freezes well, and a julienne of vegetables can be prepared – with most vegetables – a day ahead and kept in a polythene bag in the fridge.

◆ **Turkey** If you are eating at midday, the turkey can be cooked overnight in a low oven (250°F, 120°C, gas mark ½). To keep the breast moist, cook, breast down, until the last 40 minutes, then turn to brown.

◆ **Stuffing** If you are serving Chestnut and potato purée *(page 126)*, have a piquant stuffing, not sausage meat.

◆ **Accompaniments** Cook bacon rolls or cocktail sausages in the oven to save watching the grill. Bread sauce is best made a day ahead to allow time for the flavours to combine. Brown breadcrumbs give a nuttier flavour. Gravy can be made the day before, with stock and a little red wine. Don't forget to add the meat juices just before serving.

◆ **Vegetables** Green vegetables can be cooked in advance until *al dente*. Refresh immediately under cold running water to retain colour, and heat through in boiling water for 1 minute at the last moment. A vegetable purée can be made the day before and heated through at the bottom of the oven for 40

minutes. Roast potatoes are, for many, essential. Parboil them first and make sure you coat them with very hot fat. They will need to cook for an hour at the top of the oven and at a very high temperature (400°F, 200°C, gas mark 6) for the last 30 minutes. They lose their crunchiness if kept in a low oven too long.

◆ **Pudding** Christmas pudding should be made at least a month in advance. Making individual puddings cuts down cooking and reheating time. Remember to have brandy ready to flame the pudding as you bring it to the table. For those who don't like plum pudding, serve a special sorbet or ice-cream *(page 128)* with a FRUIT PURÉE.

TRADITIONAL CHRISTMAS MEAL

Clear consommé with a
julienne of vegetables
or
Grilled grapefruit

◆

Roast stuffed turkey
Cranberry sauce
Bread sauce
Bacon rolls
Brussels sprouts
Roast potatoes
or
Chestnut and potato
purée *(page 126)*

◆

Individual Christmas
puddings *(above)*
Brandy butter

Left *Flambéing in alcohol gives extra flavour to roast ham and produces a dramatic effect when done at the dinner table. Use alcohol that is at least 40° proof, such as brandy, rum or Calvados. Heat 4 tablespoons of alcohol in a ladle and set it alight with a match. Pour it, flaming, over the ham while still in · the pan and leave it to burn out.*

You really can produce from scratch something that looks and tastes good in just 15 minutes. But don't be too ambitious – it obviously must be pretty simple. There are three methods of cooking open to you: frying, grilling and boiling. This means you can use thin pieces of fish, such as fillets or cutlets, and meat such as minute steaks or veal escalopes. Fresh pasta is very quick and delicious too, as are many egg and rice dishes. In a real emergency there are even crafty ways of making tinned soup special.

If you're using the grill, turn it on before you do anything else, and warm plates and serving dishes in the oven. For frying, vegetable oil is better than butter at high temperatures. For boiling, heat water in a kettle first.

Left *Many delicious dishes can be put together quickly using store-cupboard and bought ingredients. Clockwise from the left: Pasta with cream and ham (page 106), topped with fresh, grated Parmesan – use very thin pasta or small pasta shapes as it needs to cook very quickly; minute steak with wine and cream sauce, garnished with orange segments (see above); tinned tomato soup made 'special', by adding fried chopped onion and garlic plus strained, chopped tinned tomatoes to the soup as it's heated through, and sprinkling with more fried chopped onion before serving; Soufflé omelette (page 103).*

WINE AND CREAM SAUCE

Make an instant feast using:

◆ minute steak

◆ thin fillets of white fish

◆ boned chicken breasts

◆ thin veal escalopes dusted in seasoned flour

Sauté in butter and oil for 8 minutes. Add 120 g (¼ lb) sliced mushrooms, 1 glass white wine, 2 tablespoons cream. Cover, simmer for 5 minutes, season and serve.

FAST FOODS FOR 6

◆ **Calf's liver with orange** Coat 450 g (1 lb) liver in seasoned flour. Sauté 2 chopped onions and 1 clove garlic in oil, add liver and cook for 5–8 minutes. Boil 150 ml (5 fl oz) orange juice and add chopped parsley. Pour sauce over liver.

◆ **Risotto** Boil 2 cups long-grain rice, 1 cup water and simmer, covered, until water is absorbed. Add juice of ½ lemon, 1 teaspoon turmeric, 50 g (2 oz) cooked mushrooms, and 1 can of prawns. Cook for 2 minutes.

HOW TO IMPROVE TINNED SOUP

◆ Chopped fresh herbs, sprinkled on top: basil with tomato, chives with mushroom, parsley with lentil, thyme with vegetable, mint with pea and ham

◆ Yoghurt or cream swirled on dark soups, like tomato

◆ Toasted, flaked almonds on asparagus or consommé

◆ Tinned shrimps in fish

◆ Sherry in consommé or mushroom

PASTA SAUCES

Pasta plus sauce is quick, easy, delicious and nutritious. All our suggested sauces serve 6 and should be accompanied by 575 g (1½ lb) cooked pasta. Top with fresh grated Parmesan if you can get it – the flavour is better.

◆ Make a spicy, hot sauce by heating 125 ml (5½ fl oz) olive oil, 5 peeled and sliced cloves garlic and 1½ crumbled and seeded dried chillies in a saucepan. Sauté quickly for 1 minute, add the drained pasta, cook another minute and serve.

◆ A clam sauce with tomatoes is delicious. Purée 1½ × 400 g (14 oz) tins of tomatoes. Heat 1½ tablespoons olive oil, add 3 tablespoons chopped parsley and 1½ chopped cloves garlic and cook for 2 minutes. Add the tomatoes and season. Cook for 10 minutes and add a 400 g (14 oz) tin of drained clams just before serving.

◆ Bought pesto makes a wonderful sauce. Heat through 2 tablespoons of pesto per person, mix well with the pasta and serve.

◆ For a very rich sauce try Gorgonzola and cream. Place cooked pasta in a warmed serving dish, fold in 150 g (5 oz) crumbled Gorgonzola, 50 ml (2 fl oz) single cream, and black pepper, and serve.

◆ For the classic carbonara sauce: cut 175 g (6 oz) bacon into matchsticks and fry in butter. Pour 3 beaten eggs and the drained bacon onto the cooked pasta and mix well. Add grated Parmesan and serve.

COOKING IN 30 MINUTES

The first thing to decide is whether you want to produce more than one course. If you do, it's better to bake your main course. Make sure you switch on the oven before you do anything else! Baking limits your choice but it does mean you have 10 minutes spare for vegetables or for a starter or a pudding. Don't be too ambitious; much better to be calmly within your time limit than emerging hot and flustered when the doorbell goes.

You could do *one* of the following: make a salad (either as a starter or as a SIDE SALAD), prepare and cook EASY VEGETABLES or make a FAST FRUIT PUDDING. Always try to leave yourself a couple of minutes to lay the table.

WAYS TO BAKE EGGS

Oeufs sur le plat This is a marvellously quick and easy lunch or supper dish using ingredients which can be taken from your store cupboard. The eggs are very lightly cooked, and cream or melted butter poured on top before cooking keeps the yolks soft and creamy. You can dress up the dish with two slices of smoked salmon or crab meat, or try some of our other suggestions. Another time-saving point: it's cooked as well as served in an ovenproof dish or individual shallow dishes. Melt a little butter in the dish (or dishes), add a layer of your chosen ingredients and break the eggs on top. Season, dot each yolk with a generous tablespoon of cream or a teaspoon of butter and bake at 480°F (200°C, gas mark 6) for 8 minutes.

◆ layer of chopped tinned asparagus tips

◆ 120 g (4 oz) cooked sliced mushrooms and 50 g (2 oz) cooked peas

◆ 4 tablespoons TOMATO SAUCE (or tomato purée

diluted with stock), 2 chopped anchovy fillets and few drops of olive oil

◆ sliced rashers of lean bacon and 50 g (2 oz) sliced Gruyère cheese

◆ 50 g (2 oz) grated cheese and breadcrumbs

◆ 2 cooked sausages and 1 cooked potato, both sliced

Oeufs Florentine is very similar. For this fast version break the eggs into a bed of hot cooked spinach, top with grated cheese and breadcrumbs, and bake in the oven for 10 minutes. Or try using pre-cooked pasta – tagliatelle or little shapes (bows or shells) – tossed in a light cheese sauce.

Left *Sweet and sour baked pork (page 117); lettuce and plum salad; Baked fish with tarragon (page 98); Baked chicken breasts with tomato (page 111).*

PIZZA TOPPINGS

Adding home-made toppings to pizza bases makes them far more delicious than pizzas bought complete and ready to cook. You can buy bases at most supermarkets but the packet mixes are excellent too. Spread the base with a piquant TOMATO SAUCE to within 1 cm ($\frac{1}{2}$ in) of the edge and then pile on your chosen topping. We list several suggestions below. Sprinkle with dried herbs and a little oil and bake for 20 minutes in a preheated oven at 350°F (180°C, gas mark 4).

◆ Mozzarella, basil, sliced tomato, black olives and oregano

◆ Tuna, anchovies, chopped tomatoes and black olives

◆ Chopped ham or prosciutto and chopped artichoke hearts

◆ Pepperoni and a pinch of chilli powder

◆ Chopped green peppers (blanched, if preferred) and sliced mushrooms

You could use crusty French bread instead of a pizza base. Or try Italian *crostoni*, a popular snack meal you could serve with a green salad. Thick slices of bread, are spread with soft cheese topped with prosciutto and a little oil and baked in a hot oven for 10 minutes.

TOMATO SAUCE   139

Left *Stir-fry dishes are easy to prepare and, because the food is cut into small pieces and cooks so quickly, little nutritional value is lost.* Clockwise from the top: *Stir-fried fish and green beans (page 98); Stir-fried beef and ginger (page 114); Stir-fried chicken and mango (page 113); served with boiled rice. You can also serve these dishes with Chinese noodles, which can be ready to eat in 10 minutes.*

Decide to use the top of your cooker rather than the oven for your meal in 30 minutes, and you'll have a wider choice. Go for one course and follow it very simply with cheese and fruit. Half an hour gives you time to prepare vegetables but obviously not enough time to cook them slowly, so a dish where they are cut small and cooked together with your other ingredients is ideal. This is where the wonderful wok really scores. It's a marvellously simple and quick cooking method. It's also a very healthy way of cooking food as the speed of stir-frying conserves the nutritional content. Of course, you could use a heavy-bottomed frying pan instead, but it's not as easy to handle as a wok for this type of cooking, and you'd probably have to cook the food in shifts, which rather misses the point.

USING AND LOOKING AFTER A WOK

Stainless steel woks that don't rust are available but maintaining the traditional type is easy so long as it is seasoned before first use and always wiped clean after use thereafter. To season a new wok, wash in hot water and detergent, brush with a little oil and heat gently until the oil starts to smoke. Allow the wok to cool and then wipe dry completely with absorbent kitchen paper.

The wok will come with a domed lid, to allow room for a bamboo steamer, and a circular metal support. Other accessories that you may or may not need include the following: *spatula* or stirrer with a wooden handle, for turning food; *ladle* or scoop for lifting and draining food; *draining rack*, which fits onto one side of the wok and allows cooked food to drain and stay hot while you prepare the rest; and *stand*

for steamer, usually in the shape of a wooden cross that can be placed on the bottom of the wok.

Tips

◆ Groundnut or corn oil are the best because they can be heated to a high temperature. Cut vegetables on a slant to expose the maximum surface area to heat. Slice carrots, potatoes and courgettes lengthways.

◆ Heat the wok on high, add the oil and swirl it around so that it covers the surface. Heat for a minute before adding food.

◆ Toss the food from the centre of the wok to the sides, using the spatula, to keep it moving and thus prevent burning.

◆ Add soy sauce or sesame oil seasoning at the end just before you serve.

FAST RICE DISHES

Party rice variations: using the Party rice recipe *(page 124)*, omit the almonds and add generous amounts of one of these:

◆ strips of cooked ham or pork, peas and a pinch of thyme

◆ raisins, chopped dried apricots, pine kernels and a pinch of cumin

Boiled rice variation: Mix in butter and seasoning and fluff the rice up with two forks. Add shredded pork, sultanas and a pinch of curry powder

Egg fried rice: Heat 3 tablespoons oil, add boiled rice and stir quickly. Pour in 1 beaten egg, turn heat down and blend rapidly. Add cooked peas and shelled prawns.

QUICK DISHES FOR 6

Steak or liver stroganoff Cut 450 g (1 lb) steak or calf's liver into strips. Heat 1 tablespoon oil in a frying pan and seal the meat. Remove from the pan and set aside. Reduce the heat, add sliced onion and mushrooms and cook for 2 minutes. Sprinkle in 2 tablespoons flour and stir, and then add 4 tablespoons wine and 300 ml (½ pint) sour cream, stirring well. Simmer the sauce for 2 minutes, then return the meat to the pan, warm through and serve.

◆ **Pork fillet** Grill or fry the 6 fillets in butter and serve with a BARBECUE SAUCE, adding a dash of tabasco.

◆ **Lamb chops** Rub the 6 chops with herbs, garlic and salt, and fry in a little fat or grill for 4–6 minutes on each side. Serve with mint sauce or jelly.

◆ **Hamburgers** Mix together 450 g (1 lb) ground beef, 1 chopped onion, seasoning and 1 egg. Form into six rounds and cook in 2 tablespoons hot vegetable oil or grill for 4 minutes on each side.

BARBECUE SAUCE | 138

There's a greater danger of falling into a rut with this course than with any other, and it's a good idea to make a conscious effort to add something new to your repertoire from time to time. If you know your starter is going to be straightforward to produce, delicious to eat and needs no cooking, it can be a great confidence booster. It's also good to know that the top of the cooker is not going to be cluttered with bubbling saucepans of soup, or your oven piled high with plates of quails' eggs *en croûte* keeping warm. Our suggestions have one of two advantages: either they can be prepared well ahead, or they are last-minute assembly jobs. But remember, don't put the food on the plates too early.

Left Clockwise from the left: *taramasalata served with Melba toast and olives – stiffly whisk an egg white and fold into 225 g (8 oz) taramasalata for a light, creamy texture; Chilled cucumber soup with prawns (page 94); Granary roll with ratatouille – hollow out, brush with melted butter, warm in the oven, fill with tinned ratatouille and sprinkle with Parmesan; sliced smoked chicken with horseradish, grated apple and double cream.*

BOUGHT OR SIMPLE-ASSEMBLY STARTERS

When you don't have time to prepare an elaborate starter for a supper party, buy a selection of ready-made ones, or ingredients that only need assembling. A wide variety is available from supermarkets and delicatessens. It's fun to tie in the starter with the rest of your meal and give the whole thing a national flavour.

◆ **Indian:** vegetable or meat samosas or onion bhajees, heated through and served with papadums (plain or spiced) and mango or lime chutney

◆ **Chinese:** spring rolls with chilli and soy sauce; prawn crackers with bean paste dip and hot or cold prawn and sesame toasts

◆ **Greek:** feta cheese with olives; dolmades (stuffed vine leaves); taramasalata, hummus or yoghurt and cucumber salad with pitta bread

◆ **Italian:** pepperoni sausage; prosciutto with figs or melon; tomato and Mozzarella salad; Mozzarella with dough sticks; mixed fish salad; pizza slices

◆ **French:** pâtés with French bread; French pepper salami with tomato salad; quiches (slices or individual mini ones) served hot or cold; leek vinaigrette

◆ **English:** oysters on crushed ice; smoked salmon with brown bread and lemon; cold roast beef with horseradish

◆ **Swedish:** gravlax (home-cured salmon with dill) and rye bread; pickled herrings and pickled beetroot with rye bread

◆ **Mexican:** guacamole or bean and chilli dip served with tortilla chips

◆ **Spanish:** gazpacho soup; onion, tomato and olive salad; quails' eggs

◆ **Jewish:** gefilte fish (sweet and sour fish balls) or rollmops (pickled herrings), with gherkins and rye or matzo bread

◆ **Russian:** borstch with sour cream and chives

◆ **Middle Eastern:** tabbouleh with green salad and pitta bread

AVOCADOS

◆ Avocado and Mozzarella slices: add vinaigrette and fresh parsley or walnuts and a walnut oil dressing.

◆ Guacamole (for 6): blend 3 avocados, 1 onion, 2 cloves garlic, lemon juice, oil, 2 tomatoes, dash of tabasco and 1 chilli.

◆ Mix flesh of 3 halved avocados with lemon juice, 150 ml (5 fl oz) yoghurt and 175 g (6 oz) cooked chicken. Season and refill shells. (Serves 6.)

FRUIT STARTERS

◆ Toss fresh sliced pears in STILTON DRESSING and top with chopped walnuts

◆ Toss fresh sliced pineapple in FRENCH DRESSING and serve with cottage cheese and flaked almonds

◆ Toss diced melon, tomato and seedless black grapes in LEMON AND MINT DRESSING and top with fresh mint

◆ Toss segments of orange, shredded Chinese cabbage, watercress and celery in VINAIGRETTE

SIDE SALADS

There are two secrets to the making of a good salad: use it fresh and keep it dry. Buy the freshest ingredients – or grow your own – and store at the bottom of your fridge. When you wash leaves, wrap them gently in a cloth and whirl it round your head or use a salad spinner.

Don't use too many ingredients; you can make a really good salad from just three. Cut your vegetables into interesting shapes – julienne strips of carrot or celery look more attractive and seem to taste better too. Make your dressing in advance so the flavours have time to combine. If using cooked ingredients, add the dressing while they are still warm. Pulses make your salads more filling – tinned, red kidney beans are very quick and taste wonderful. Alternatives are rice, pasta, potatoes and bulgar wheat.

Right Clockwise from the left: *mushroom, chive and black olive salad with Roquefort and sour cream dressing; pink grapefruit, mange-tout and curly endive with a raspberry dressing; red and green salad of French and kidney beans, layered with lettuce and radicchio, garnished with garlic mayonnaise; oriental salad of shredded Chinese cabbage, beansprouts and sliced baby sweetcorn in a sesame oil dressing; lamb's lettuce with grated carrot and celeriac, sprinkled with toasted sunflower seeds.*

SALADS WITH MAYONNAISE

You may not have time to make home-made mayonnaise, but some of the bought ones are very good. You can add extra ingredients: a pinch of curry or saffron powder makes a spicy yellow mayonnaise; a dash of tomato ketchup and Worcester sauce makes a 'prawn cocktail' dressing; and fresh chopped herbs or garlic are delicious. Try your own combinations: here are a few of ours.

◆ Shrimps, celery and chicory with curried mayonnaise

◆ Cooked white fish and mange-tout with saffron mayonnaise

◆ Grated celeriac and horseradish with plain mayonnaise

◆ Red kidney beans, sliced raw onions and tomatoes with dill mayonnaise

SALAD TOPPINGS

You can add texture, flavour and decoration to any simple salad in no time.

◆ Sunflower seeds over sliced chicory and mushrooms

◆ Salami shapes on lettuce and grated carrot

◆ Hot diced bacon and spring onion over spinach

◆ Toasted almonds on blanched mange-tout and French beans

◆ Garlic croûtons on radicchio

SALADS WITH OIL AND VINEGAR

For me a salad without dressing loses half its charm. French dressing is 1 part white wine vinegar to 3–5 parts olive oil, to which French mustard, crushed garlic, seasoning and herbs are added. Vinaigrette omits mustard. Experiment with the balance of oil to vinegar – I like mine quite sharp and often add a little lemon juice. Try different oils and vinegars: walnut and hazelnut oils have strong flavours, whereas sunflower and safflower oils are more delicate; herb or fruit vinegars give a tangy flavour. For a sweeter dressing, I admit to sometimes adding sugar.

◆ Combine raspberry vinegar, sunflower oil, herbs and seasoning for green salad with grapes.

◆ Combine 3–4 tablespoons sesame oil with 1 tablespoon soy sauce and 1 tablespoon honey for bean sprouts and raw vegetables.

◆ Combine tarragon vinegar, mixture of safflower and walnut oils and seasonings for peaches, cottage cheese, chicory and lettuce.

◆ Combine hazelnut and sunflower oils with unsweetened grape juice and seasonings for lettuce, sliced plums and chicory.

EASY VEGETABLES

There are many opinions on the best way to cook vegetables, but certainly most people would agree that they should never be overcooked, but served *al dente* or slightly crisp. I was taught that those grown above the ground should be plunged into boiling water and cooked without a lid, and root vegetables should be brought to a boil, then covered while simmering. Easier ways to cook them, neither of which depend on such crucial timing, are BRAISING and steaming, and both have the advantage of retaining more vitamins. Braising is useful for entertaining: once you've put the vegetables in the oven they cook themselves, and they are especially good with drier meats because their liquid can replace gravy.

Left Clockwise from the top *Two-tone cabbage (page 124); Braised fennel (page 125); cabbage leaves filled with Party rice (page 124); Parsnip and pear purée (page 126) and carrot purée; Leek and tomato gratin (page 124); Courgette boats (page 123) with Tomato sauce (page 139).*

HOW TO STEAM VEGETABLES

Steaming is an immensely satisfying way of cooking vegetables. Suspended in a container over a little boiling water, it's difficult to overcook them and they keep their colour and texure beautifully while losing less of their vitamins.

Different types of steamers are available. Steaming baskets just sit in the saucepan: you can improvise with a metal colander. At the other end of the price scale, oval baskets

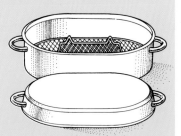

a higher tier, or later on if you are using a simple basket. Cover tightly. Steaming takes 3–5 minutes longer than boiling. Top up with water if the pan starts to boil dry and add herbs for extra flavour.

You can cook vegetables of a similar cooking time together. Root vegetables should be sliced lengthwise and cooked in layers. Dark-green leafy vegetables, such as spinach, don't steam well and are better boiled in a little water.

can steam a fish and several vegetables together. There are tiered steamers made cheaply in BAMBOO or, more expensively, in metal.

Bring the water to a boil before adding the vegetables. Put those that take the longest, like potatoes, at the bottom; those that cook more quickly, like sliced courgettes, can be added to

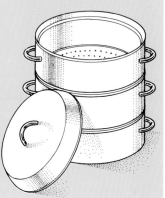

SAUCES AND GLAZES

◆ **Cheese sauce** (for 6): Melt 50 g (2 oz) butter and add 3 tablespoons flour; add 450 ml (¾ pint) milk and seasoning and thicken. Add 50 g (2 oz) cheese and grated nutmeg. Serve with leeks, broccoli or spinach.

◆ **Béchamel sauce:** As above, but omit cheese and flavour milk with onion, 4 peppercorns and mace. Serve with courgettes.

◆ **Glazed carrots** (for 6): Cover 675 g (1½ lb) sliced carrots with water; add little butter, 1 teaspoon sugar and black pepper. Simmer till liquid has reduced.

SKINNING PEPPERS

Peppers are sweeter and more digestible without their skins. Grill them until they blister all over or, better still, char them over a gas flame spreader. Pop them immediately into a plastic bag and seal the top for 30 seconds. When you take them out and wash them under running water you will find that the skins come off very easily.

FAST FRUIT PUDDINGS

Right *Iced pears filled with bought sorbet or home-made Champagne sorbet (page 128). Cut off the tops of 6 slightly under-ripe pears and put them in water with a little lemon juice added to prevent discolouring. Hollow out the pears and add them to the acidulated water. Make a syrup with water and sugar, add the pears and lids and simmer for 2 minutes. Drain and chill. When ready to serve, fill the pears with frozen sorbet and replace the lids.*

FRUIT PURÉES

Fruit purées are a wonderful accompaniment to ice-cream, sorbet, yoghurt, goat's cheese or slices of fresh fruit. Raspberry purée is delicious with crème fraîche or a soft, creamy cheese such as chèvre, for instance. Good fruits for puréeing include strawberries, peaches, apricots, gooseberries, raspberries, blackberries and blueberries, mangoes and kiwi fruit. Try contrasting colours for special effect: serve red purée with green fruit or vanilla ice-cream, golden purée with chocolate mousse. Begin by puréeing the fruit in a blender or food processor (with a little icing sugar to keep the colour), adding a little sweet wine to get the consistency you want, if necessary, and then pass the fruit through a sieve. The purée can be made just before a meal, or in advance and stored in the fridge or freezer, but remember to allow time for defrosting.

Fresh fruit is the perfect pudding: colourful, healthy and quick. If you want to make an effort, a fresh fruit salad using three carefully chosen ingredients is always successful. In summer, of course, the choice is enormous. In winter it's more limited but don't forget dried fruit, particularly the type you don't have to soak, and dates, figs and nuts. Many tropical fruits are now widely available. Be aware of colour as well as taste when choosing your fruits, and don't make the salad too far ahead or it will lose its freshness. A little mint or a dash of alcohol sprinkled over it is delicious. For something a little more unusual combine sorbets with fruit: fruit purées (or coulis) look rather special. Or flambé your fruit — not difficult and always a treat.

FRUIT BRÛLÉES

Use several fruits – oranges, bananas and grapes, or peaches and raspberries – or just one type, such as apricots, strawberries or blueberries. The basic cooking method is the same. Slice the fruit, removing any stones; add some liqueur (optional) and completely cover the fruit with whipped double cream or yoghurt. Sprinkle with brown sugar, preferably demerara, and place under a hot grill for 3 minutes, until the sugar caramelizes.

FRUIT IN ALCOHOL

Fruits steeped or cooked in 2 tablespoons of alcohol (wine or liqueur) develop a deliciously rich flavour.

◆ Purée mangoes, oranges and Cointreau. Stir in yoghurt and serve with orange slices.

◆ Add Kirsch and white wine to a salad of kiwi fruit, green grapes and melon.

◆ Flambé bananas by gently heating orange juice, sugar and butter together and then add sliced bananas and brandy or rum, set alight and serve with juices.

Above left *Pastry fruit squares make attractive individual desserts. Peeled, cored apple halves work particularly well – see Apple square puffs (page 133) – but you could use other similar fruit, such as pears, or even peaches and apricots.*
Below left *A bought sponge ring filled with lightly poached grapes and orange segments, flambéed with brandy or Cointreau.*

APPETIZERS

MUSHROOM OR PRAWN CROÛTES

Illustrated on page 35

Makes 8

8 slices one-day-old white bread
85 g (3 oz) melted butter
8 button mushrooms, or 16 prawns

I'd always rather not deep-fry, and this method is very successful. The croûtes are also good with garlic and anchovy butter, or anchor the prawns or mushrooms with a mayonnaise salad topping.

Heat the oven to 400°F (200°C, gas mark 6). Cut the white bread into small heart shapes or circles. Brush both sides with melted butter and place in the oven for 5 minutes, or until golden coloured. Place a mushroom, or two prawns, on each croûte and cook for another 2−3 minutes. The mushrooms or prawns should be hot and the croûtes crisp.

Preparation time: 5 minutes
Cooking time: 8 minutes

SESAME BALLS

Illustrated on page 36

Makes 24

120 g (4 oz) sesame seeds
120 g (4 oz) sunflower seeds
120 g (4 oz) pumpkin seeds
120 g (4 oz) full-fat feta cheese
4 teaspoons soy sauce
4 teaspoons sesame oil
2 egg whites

These are so easy that they would be worth making as snacks to go with drinks or on picnics as a very nutritious and tasty change from crisps and peanuts.

Heat the oven to 400°F (200°C, gas mark 6). Spread the sesame seeds on a baking tray and toast in the preheated oven for a few minutes until browned, then transfer to a bowl.
   In a food processor, process the sunflower seeds and pumpkin seeds (or use a pestle and mortar) until they are almost smooth. Blend in the feta cheese, soy sauce and sesame oil until smooth. Take a spoonful of the mixture and form into a bite-sized ball, then roll it in the egg white and the sesame seeds. Repeat with the remaining mixture. Place the sesame balls in the fridge. Remove half an hour before needed and serve on a bed of lettuce leaves.

Advance preparation: The sesame balls can be made a few hours in advance and stored in the fridge, but if left overnight they tend to dry out.
Preparation time: 15−20 minutes

AVOCADO DIP

Illustrated on page 48

Serves 6

3−4 sorrel leaves (or ½ bunch watercress leaves)
1 large ripe avocado
1 tablespoon lemon juice
2 tablespoons sour cream or Greek yoghurt
salt and black pepper

Make sure you use really ripe avocados to give the fullest possible taste. And have a selection of crisp, raw vegetables to eat it with: slices of carrot, pepper, courgette, pieces of cauliflower and endive.

Wash and dry the sorrel or watercress leaves and blend to a purée. Add the flesh of the avocado (scraping close to the skin as this gives the dip its lovely colour). Then add the other ingredients and blend until smooth.

Advance preparation: Avocado flesh discolours quite quickly in contact with the air, so the dip should be made on the day you intend to serve it. You can always scoop off the top layer at the last minute, as this won't affect the taste.
Preparation time: 10 minutes

CREAM CHEESE AND HERB DIP

Serves 6

175 g (6 oz) cream cheese
2−4 tablespoons sour cream
1 tablespoon creamed horseradish
2 tablespoons each fresh tarragon, chervil and parsley
salt and black pepper

This lovely dip is so wonderfully easy to make and can be used on all sorts of different occasions. You could substitute tomato ketchup for the horseradish if you're making it for young children: they might prefer the slightly blander flavour. Serve it with crunchy pieces of vegetable or some good crisps or little savoury biscuits.

Finely chop the herbs. Mix the ingredients together and season well. If you can't find fresh tarragon and chervil, soak a tablespoon each of the dried variety in lemon juice for a couple of hours before adding to the mixture.

Preparation time: 8 minutes

FILO PASTRY TRIANGLES

Illustrated on page 50

Serves 6

6 sheets filo pastry
melted butter

Note: *The secret of good filo is to brush each and every layer with butter. If there is not enough butter, the under layers tend to remain uncooked and it is then very indigestible.*

Filo is easy to handle, light to eat and can be used for sweet or savoury dishes. You can buy it frozen in 450 g (1 lb) packets, which contain at least 24 sheets. Keep it in the freezer, transferring it to the fridge 12 hours before you want to use it. You can make all sorts of differently shaped parcels, from traditional triangles to mini crackers. Don't refreeze any left over; return to the fridge, sealed in its original package. It will keep for a month.

Heat the oven to 350°F (180°C, gas mark 4). Unwrap the filo and count out six sheets. Separate one, and roll up the others, covering with a damp cloth until ready to use. Return the rest to the packet and place in the fridge. Take the filo sheet, brush it with melted butter and cut it into four strips, 6.3 cm × 25.4 cm (2½ in × 10 in). Lay a small teaspoon of the filling in one corner of a strip and fold the corner over to make a triangle. Fold the strip over again and again, each time making a triangle. Brush with melted butter as you wrap, sticking down the ends, and place the triangle on a baking sheet. Do the same with another strip. Continue until you have used all six sheets. Cook in the preheated oven for 15–20 minutes, or until golden brown. Serve immediately.

Advance preparation: Filled, uncooked, filo parcels can be stored in the refrigerator for a day before they are required or in the freezer for longer periods. In either case, prepare them but don't brush the outside layers with butter until ready to use. If freezing, place on a baking tray and, when they are frozen, pack in plastic bags. When you want to use them, put them on a buttered baking tray, brush with butter and put them in the oven immediately as they go soggy when defrosted. Cook at 350°F (180°C, gas mark 4) for 45 minutes, or until browned. Serve immediately.
Preparation time: 20 minutes
Cooking time: 45 minutes

Anchovy Filling

225 g (½ lb) white fish fillets
4 anchovy fillets
3 tablespoons parsley, finely chopped
salt and black pepper

Finely chop or blend the fish and anchovy and mix with the parsley. Season with salt and freshly ground black pepper.

Preparation time: 10 minutes

Mushroom Filling

225 g (½ lb) mushrooms
25 g (1 oz) butter
120 g (4 oz) cream cheese
salt and black pepper

Finely chop the mushrooms. Melt the butter in the pan and add the mushrooms. Cook for about 10 minutes, stirring occasionally, until all the moisture has evaporated. Remove from the heat and allow to cool a little. Blend the mushrooms and cream cheese thoroughly, and season with salt and freshly ground black pepper.

Preparation and cooking time: 20 minutes

Spinach Filling

225 g (½ lb) frozen chopped spinach
25 g (1 oz) butter, softened
120 g (4 oz) cream cheese
salt and black pepper
nutmeg

Defrost the spinach in a saucepan, over a medium heat, stirring regularly. Continue to cook until the water has completely evaporated. Finely chop the spinach, either by hand or using a food processor. Add the softened butter and the cream cheese, season to taste with salt and freshly ground black pepper and then add a generous pinch of nutmeg. Blend until well mixed.

Preparation and cooking time: 20 minutes

STARTERS

TOMATO AND BASIL SORBET

Illustrated on page 73

Serves 6

50 g (2 oz) glucose
120 g (4 oz) caster sugar
300 ml (½ pint) water
400 g (14 oz) can tomatoes
juice of ½ lemon
2 tablespoons white wine
2–3 drops tabasco
salt and black pepper
2 tablespoons finely
    chopped basil

This delicious savoury sorbet would make an unusual first course served with hot toast or a refreshing break mid-meal — especially between two rich courses. In either case, a little goes a long way. Don't forget to transfer it from the freezer to the fridge well before serving or it will be too hard.

Place the glucose in a heavy-based saucepan, add the sugar and water and bring slowly to the boil, so that the sugar dissolves. Simmer for 5 minutes, and then allow the syrup to cool completely.

Meanwhile, blend the remaining ingredients (except the basil) in the liquidizer. Pour into a freezer-proof container. When the syrup is cold, add it, with the basil, to the tomatoes, mix and transfer to the freezer. The sorbet takes 6–8 hours to freeze so it should be stirred with a fork every couple of hours to break down the water crystals. Remove from the freezer half an hour before serving.

Preparation time: 30 minutes
Freezing time: 8 hours

MARINATED BRIE

Illustrated on page 15

Serves 6

240 g (¾ lb) Brie, cut into 6
    slices
150 ml (¼ pint) olive oil
1 teaspoon dried basil
10 black peppercorns
2 cloves garlic, sliced
mâche (lamb's lettuce) to
    serve

Note: *For more than six people, allow at least 50 g (2 oz) Brie per person, and make enough marinade to cover the cheese.*

As well as an unusual and elegant starter, this would make a good basis for a vegetarian salad — a welcome change from a slab of Cheddar. The longer you leave it to marinate, the stronger the taste will be.

Cook the basil, peppercorns and sliced garlic in the oil until it starts to bubble. Don't overcook as the garlic will burn. Remove the pan from the heat and allow to cool.

Place the sliced Brie on the bottom of a shallow dish and pour over the marinade, so that the cheese is covered. Leave to stand for

at least 4 hours before serving.

To serve, arrange two or three slices of cheese on the salad leaves and dribble over the marinade. Add the marinade at the last minute so that the salad does not become limp.

Advance preparation: The cheese can be stored in the refrigerator for up to two days. Bring out at least 2–4 hours before it is needed, so that it can be served at room temperature.
Preparation time: 10 minutes
Marinating time: at least 4 hours

DUCK BREAST SALAD WITH BLACKCURRANT SAUCE

Illustrated on page 25

Serves 6

2 large duck breasts
1 × 275 g (10 oz) tin
    blackcurrants
2 tablespoons redcurrant
    jelly
1 tablespoon cornflour
1 tablespoon lemon juice
radicchio and curly endive
3 tablespoons walnut oil
1 tablespoon red wine
    vinegar
salt and black pepper

What a smart starter! Or it would make an exotic centrepiece with a more substantial salad for a lunch party. You could grill the meat if you prefer.

Place the duck breasts, skin side down, in the frying pan without fat or oil. Cook over a moderate heat until the skin crisps and the natural fat has come out — about 8 minutes. Drain off most of the fat, turn the duck breasts over and cook for a further 5 minutes on the other side. Remove from the pan and set aside.

To make the sauce, strain the blackcurrant juice into a saucepan, reserving the black-currants. Add the redcurrant jelly and bring to a boil, stirring well until the jelly has melted. Dissolve the cornflour in the lemon juice and add this to the boiling liquid. Cook until the sauce has thickened, then remove the pan from

the heat and add the blackcurrants.

Clean the radicchio and curly endive leaves well and place in the fridge, in a plastic bag, until ready to use. Mix the walnut oil and red wine vinegar and add seasoning. To serve, place some salad leaves at the side of each plate and sprinkle a little walnut dressing over them. Remove the fat from the duck and cut each breast into six slices lengthways. Arrange the slices on the plate in a fan which just touches the salad leaves. Spoon a little sauce onto each plate, but not over the meat, and serve.

Advance preparation: The dish can be cooked in advance, but it should be assembled at the last minute.
Preparation and cooking time: 25 minutes

LAYERED AVOCADO AND TOMATO MOUSSE

Illustrated on page 24

Serves 6–8

3 ripe avocados
300 ml (½ pint) double
     cream
2 × 15 g (½ oz) packet
     powdered gelatine
lemon juice
salt and black pepper
2 egg whites
200 g (7 oz) tin chopped
     tomato
425 g (15 oz) tin consommé
1 clove garlic
2 tablespoons tomato purée

Note: *If you are worried that
the gelatine will not set, try
the recipe the first time with
only two layers.*

*The classic combination of creamy avocado and
piquant tomato is delicious in this dish, which
looks complicated but isn't. To show it off to best
advantage, make it in a loaf tin and serve in slices.*

Cut the avocados in half, remove the stones,
scoop out the flesh and blend. When it is
smooth, add the double cream and mix
thoroughly. Dissolve 15 g (½ oz) powdered
gelatine in three tablespoons cold water,
following the manufacturer's instructions. When
the gelatine has dissolved, add it to the avocado
mixture. Add lemon juice and seasoning and
transfer to a mixing bowl. In a separate bowl,
whisk the egg whites until stiff and fold them
into the avocado mixture. Wet a 1.6 litre (3 pint)
loaf tin, or ring mould, and pour in half the
avocado mixture. Put the tin in the fridge to set.

Combine the chopped tomato and consommé
in a bowl. Finely chop the garlic and add it, with
seasoning. Mix 2 tablespoons of tomato purée
in 3 tablespoons cold water and add to the
tomato consommé. Dissolve the remaining 15 g
(½oz) gelatine, following the manufacturer's
instructions, add it to the tomato mixture and
place in the fridge. When the avocado mixture in
the fridge has set, pour the tomato mixture on
top, and when this sets, add the remaining
avocado mixture.

Preparation time: 40 minutes
Setting time: 2–3 hours

SPINACH MOUSSE

Illustrated on page 73

Serves 6

225 g (½ lb) frozen chopped
     spinach
oil for greasing
3 eggs
150 ml (¼ pint) single cream
4 tablespoons double cream
25 g (1 oz) Cheddar cheese,
     grated
salt and black pepper
nutmeg (preferably freshly
     grated)
150 ml (¼ pint) sour cream

Note: *It is always better to
use freshly grated nutmeg –
the flavour is much stronger.*

*Serve this hot or cold as a starter – or cooked in
one large container for about an hour as an
accompanying vegetable.*

Heat the oven to 350°F (180°C, gas mark 4).
Cut circles out of greaseproof paper and place
them in the base of six 150 ml (¼ pint) ramekin
dishes or dariole moulds. Brush the base and
sides of the dishes with oil.

Defrost the spinach and squeeze out all the
excess liquid. The spinach should not weigh
more than 150 g (5 oz) at this point.

Finely chop the spinach by hand or in a
food processor. Add the eggs, cream, grated
cheese, seasoning and nutmeg. Mix well and
pour into the moulds. Put the moulds in a
bain-marie, with enough water to come two
thirds of the way up the moulds. Bake in the
preheated oven for 30 minutes, or until the
mixture has risen and is coming away from the
sides of the moulds. Test by inserting a skewer
in the middle of the mixture; it should come
out clean. Turn the moulds onto six warmed
plates and serve with a little sour cream.

Advance preparation: The mousse can be
kept in the fridge uncooked for a day.
Preparation and cooking time: 40 minutes

SPINACH SOUFFLÉ CRÊPES

Serves 6

12 crêpes (see batter recipe,
     page 131)
225 g (8 oz) puréed fresh or
     frozen spinach
40 g (1½ oz) butter
salt and black pepper
generous pinch nutmeg
50 g (2 oz) plain flour
300 ml (½ pint) hot milk
4 eggs, separated
30 g (1 oz) grated Gruyère
     or Parmesan cheese

*A light, fluffy variation on the popular stuffed
pancake as a starter or very light main course.*

Butter a large ovenproof dish, then heat the
oven to 400°F (200°C, gas mark 6).

Put the spinach into a thick-bottomed
saucepan with a nut of butter, salt, pepper and
nutmeg and cook until the moisture has
evaporated. Melt the remaining butter in
another pan, stir in the flour and cook for a
minute or two. Remove the pan from the heat
and add the hot milk, stirring all the time.
When it is absorbed, cook very gently for 5
minutes. Remove from the heat, add the
spinach mixture and beat in the egg yolks.

Whisk the egg whites until stiff but not dry
and fold them into the spinach with a metal
spoon. Heap the mixture onto one half of each
crêpe, sprinkle with cheese and fold over.
Place the crêpes side by side in an ovenproof
dish and bake them in the preheated oven for
12–15 minutes. Serve the crêpes as soon as
they are ready.

Preparation time: 15 minutes
Cooking time: 15 minutes

GRILLED RADICCHIO

Serves 6

450 g (1 lb) radicchio, halved
3 tablespoons olive oil
black pepper
50 g (2 oz) mushrooms
2 tablespoons lemon juice
12 slices goat's cheese
1 bunch watercress
1 tablespoon finely chopped
    parsley

The mild bitterness and intense colour of radicchio have made it a popular raw salad ingredient, but here it is given a new twist – it is brushed with olive oil and lightly grilled, then mixed with slices of goat's cheese, mushrooms and watercress.

Heat the grill. Brush the radicchio with olive oil and sprinkle with freshly ground black pepper. Slice the mushrooms and coat with lemon juice.

Cook the radicchio under the hot grill for a few minutes on each side, turning regularly. Serve a few leaves on individual plates with the goat's cheese, the watercress and the sliced mushrooms. Sprinkle with the chopped parsley.

Preparation time: 15 minutes
Cooking time: 5 minutes

STUFFED ARTICHOKES

Serves 6

6 medium globe artichokes
175 g (6 oz) fresh wholemeal
    breadcrumbs
85 g (3 oz) Parmesan cheese,
    finely grated
¾ teaspoon dried oregano
3 cloves garlic, finely chopped
1 large onion, finely chopped
6 tablespoons chopped parsley
2 lemons
black pepper
4 tablespoons olive oil
melted butter or vinaigrette

A garlicky stuffing of Parmesan cheese, breadcrumbs, onion and herbs is the perfect complement to globe artichokes. Melted butter or vinaigrette provides the finishing touch.

Remove the stalk and the outer old leaves from the artichokes. Grate 2 teaspoons lemon rind. In a bowl, mix the breadcrumbs, Parmesan cheese, oregano, garlic, onion, parsley, lemon rind and freshly ground black pepper to taste. Spread the leaves of each artichoke and fill the spaces with the breadcrumb mixture.

Put the artichokes in a saucepan just large enough to hold them upright – you may need two saucepans. Pour the olive oil over the artichokes. Add enough water to come halfway up the sides of the artichokes and

add the remaining lemon rind cut into strips. Bring the water to a boil and simmer, covered, for 35–45 minutes, or until the outer leaves of the artichokes can be easily removed.

Remove the artichokes from the water and serve hot or at room temperature, with melted butter or vinaigrette if desired.

Preparation time: 45 minutes
Cooking time: 45–55 minutes

RICOTTA AND HAM BALLS

Serves 6

225 g (8 oz) low-fat ricotta
    cheese
120 g (4 oz) sliced smoked
    ham, diced
6 tablespoons finely chopped
    parsley
1 egg
grated nutmeg
salt and black pepper
85–120 g (3–4 oz) fine dry
    breadcrumbs, toasted
4 tablespoons finely grated
    Parmesan cheese
vegetable oil
lettuce to garnish
tomato sauce and pesto sauce

With their crisp coating and creamy insides, these make a very appetizing start to a meal. Accompany them with a choice of sauces such as pesto and tomato.

In a bowl, blend together the ricotta cheese, smoked ham, parsley, egg, and nutmeg, salt and pepper to taste. Shape into 12 balls. Mix together the breadcrumbs and Parmesan cheese. Use to coat the cheese balls. Heat the vegetable oil in a frying pan and shallow fry the cheese balls a few at a time for 2 minutes. Remove from the frying pan and drain on paper towels.

Place 2 balls on each plate, with the lettuce, and serve immediately with a choice of pesto sauce and tomato sauce.

Advance preparation: The cheese balls can be shaped and coated with the cheese and breadcrumb mixture, then kept, covered, in the refrigerator until ready to fry and serve.
Preparation time: 20 minutes
Cooking time: 4–6 minutes

CARPACCIO

Serves 6

175 g (6 oz) fillet of beef in one piece
12 Greek olives, stoned and chopped
1 tablespoon capers
1 clove garlic, finely chopped
4 tablespoons olive oil
1 Lollo Rosso lettuce
salt and black pepper
2 tablespoons Parmesan cheese shavings

This traditional Italian starter couldn't be simpler to make, but its success depends on using the best-quality ingredients – beef, olives, olive oil and Parmesan cheese.

Chill the fillet of beef, well wrapped, in the freezer for 2–3 hours until nearly frozen. Combine the olives, capers, garlic and olive oil in a small bowl.

Remove the fillet and cut it into 12 paper-thin slices. Pound individual slices between sheets of cling film and store in the refrigerator until ready to use. Arrange the lettuce on six plates and place the beef fillet slices beside the lettuce. Season with salt and black pepper, and spoon over the olive oil mixture. Top the beef fillet slices with cheese shavings and serve.

Advance preparation: The beef can be sliced and pounded and the olive mixture can be prepared several hours ahead. Add the Parmesan just before serving.
Preparation time: 25 minutes
Chilling time: 2–3 hours

QUAIL'S EGG SALAD

Serves 6

12 quail's eggs
½ head curly endive (frisée)
2 heads chicory
2–3 radicchio leaves
2 tablespoons lemon juice
6 tablespoons olive oil
salt and black pepper
3 tablespoons croûtons

Note: *This also tastes extremely good with cooked chopped bacon.*

Tiny quail's eggs and crunchy croûtons turn this colourful salad into a special first course. The eggs are only half peeled so you can appreciate the pretty speckled shells.

Put the quail's eggs in a saucepan of cold water, bring to a boil and then drain at once and run under cold water. Immediately peel off half the shell, leaving the other half on the rounded end of the eggs. (If you do not do this while the eggs are still hot, they are very difficult to peel.)

Clean and prepare the salad leaves. Whisk together the lemon juice and olive oil, and season with salt and black pepper. Arrange the salad leaves on six plates, add the quail's eggs and sprinkle with the croûtons. When ready to serve, pour on the olive oil dressing.

Preparation time: 20 minutes
Cooking time: 3–5 minutes

CURRIED PRAWNS WITH GRAPES

Serves 6

450 g (1 lb) seedless green grapes
450 g (1 lb) cooked prawns
85 g (3 oz) chopped walnuts
150 ml (¼ pint) sour cream
150 ml (¼ pint) mayonnaise
1–2 teaspoons finely chopped fresh root ginger
1–2 teaspoons curry powder
1–2 tablespoons lemon juice
crisp lettuce to serve

The creamy dressing for this salad of prawns, grapes and walnuts is lightly spiced with curry powder and fresh root ginger. The combination is quite irresistible.

Cut the grapes in half if they are large. Mix together the shelled prawns, grapes and chopped walnuts, leaving a few walnuts aside to garnish.

Mix together the remaining ingredients to make the dressing and then fold in the prawn mixture. Chill for several hours.

Serve the curried prawns on a bed of crisp lettuce, garnished with the remaining chopped walnuts.

Preparation time: 15 minutes plus chilling

SOUPS

ICED AVOCADO SOUP

Serves 6

2 ripe avocados
1 teaspoon chopped chives
  or minced onion
6 tablespoons lemon juice
750 ml (1¼ pint) chicken
  stock
1 × 150 g (5 oz) carton
  natural yoghurt
2 tablespoons single cream
  or sour cream
salt and black pepper

This was one of the first starters I ever made – and I still think it's one of the easiest and most successful. Make sure the avocados are ripe or it will be tasteless – it's always safest to buy them several days, even a week, in advance, if you can. Serve it with pieces of crisp Melba toast.

Scoop the flesh from the avocados and blend it with the chives (or onion) and the lemon juice until smooth. Add the remaining ingredients,

blend again and season to taste. Transfer to a bowl, cover with cling film, and chill in the fridge until ready to serve.

Advance preparation: This soup needs to be made on the day as it will discolour. Remove the top layer before serving.
Preparation time: 10–15 minutes

CHILLED CUCUMBER SOUP WITH PRAWNS

Illustrated on page 80

Serves 6

1 large cucumber
1 clove garlic, crushed
150 ml (¼ pint) single cream
1 × 150 g (5 oz) carton
  natural yoghurt
2 tablespoons white wine
1 tablespoon chopped mint
½ teaspoon dried tarragon
300 ml (½ pint) shelled
  prawns
salt and black pepper

The prawns add an elegant touch, but it's quite good enough to serve without them for a simpler occasion. Make sure it's really cold, and float very thin slices of cucumber on top at the last minute if you like.

Peel and grate the cucumber quite coarsely. Combine all the ingredients in a large bowl and mix well. Season to taste and chill in the fridge until ready to serve.

Advance preparation: If you make the soup the previous day, add the prawns and mint just before serving.
Preparation time: 10 minutes

MUSHROOM SOUP

Serves 6

340 g (12 oz) mushrooms,
  cleaned
juice of half a lemon
45 g (1½ oz) butter
45 g (1½ oz) flour
750 ml (1¼ pints) chicken
  stock
300 ml (½ pint) milk
150 ml (¼ pint) double
  cream
salt and black pepper

Mushroom soup is always popular and I love the velvety texture of this version – it's a good alternative to Almond soup (page 95) for a late-night supper. Sprinkle with chopped fresh herbs just before serving.

Purée the mushrooms and add the lemon juice. Melt the butter and add the flour, stirring constantly. Gradually add the chicken stock and half the milk, bring to a boil and reduce to

a simmer. Add the remainder of the milk and puréed mushrooms. Simmer for 10 minutes, then add the double cream and seasoning.

Advance preparation: Make the soup but add the cream and seasoning just before serving.
Preparation and cooking time: 30 minutes

PUMPKIN SOUP

Serves 6

1.4 kg (3 lb) pumpkin
600 ml (1 pint) milk
½–1 teaspoon ground cumin
½–1 teaspoon ground
  coriander
salt and black pepper
150 ml (¼ pint) sour cream
croûtons to serve
chopped parsley to serve

A lovely, rich, filling soup – you'd only need a light course to follow. It's the perfect way to use up the flesh from your Hallowe'en lantern!

Remove the skin and seeds from the pumpkin and coarsely chop the flesh. Place in a saucepan with the milk and cook for 20–30 minutes until the pumpkin is soft.
  Blend the pumpkin, together with the milk,

in a liquidizer as it gives a better finish, and return it to the saucepan. Add the spices, and season to taste. Stir in the sour cream and serve with croûtons and chopped parsley.

Preparation time: 5 minutes
Cooking time: 35 minutes

WATERCRESS SOUP

Serves 6

2 bunches watercress
225 g (½ lb) potatoes
2 onions, chopped
50 g (2 oz) butter
150 ml (¼ pint) dry white
    wine
1.2 litres (2 pints) chicken
    stock
150 ml (¼ pint) single cream
salt and black pepper

*Adding the raw watercress after the soup is cooked
makes it a lovely emerald colour. For a family
occasion, use milk instead of cream and wine.*

Cut off the watercress stalks and put the
leaves of one bunch aside until ready to use.
Keep a few good leaves for garnishing. Peel
the potatoes and cut them into quarters. Melt
the butter in a large saucepan and cook the
onions until soft, but not brown. Add the
potatoes, all the stalks and the leaves of one
bunch of watercress, and the wine. Bring to a
boil and add the chicken stock. Cook for
10−15 minutes, or until the potatoes are soft.
Allow the soup to cool a little before adding
the leaves of the second bunch, then blend
until smooth. Return the soup to the saucepan
and cook for a couple of minutes but do not
allow the soup to boil again.

Season to taste, add the cream and heat
through. Serve garnished with watercress.

Preparation time: 10 minutes
Cooking time: 20 minutes

ALMOND SOUP

Illustrated on page 48

Serves 6

225 g (8 oz) unblanched
    almonds
45 g (1½ oz) butter
45 g (1½ oz) flour
900 ml (1½ pints) chicken
    stock
1 clove garlic, crushed
300 ml (½ pint) single cream
salt and black pepper
chopped chives

*This is a very unusual and subtle soup. Serve it
either hot or cold and sprinkle with a few chives if
you think it looks bland. Blanching and chopping
is boring, but it does help the flavour to use whole
almonds.*

Blanch, peel and chop the almonds. Melt the
butter and add the flour, stirring constantly, to
form a roux. Gradually add the stock, bring to
a boil and allow to simmer for a minute or
two. Add the crushed garlic and chopped
almonds and continue to simmer for 20
minutes. Allow to cool.

Blend the soup until smooth and return to
the saucepan. Add the cream and seasoning.
Decorate with chopped chives.

Advance preparation: The soup can be made
in advance and chilled in the fridge.
Preparation and cooking time: 40 minutes

CREAM OF SCALLOP SOUP

Serves 6

½ lb (225 g) scallops
30 g (1 oz) butter
30 g (1 oz) flour
300 ml (½ pint) fish or
    chicken stock
300 ml (½ pint) milk
150 ml (¼ pint) double
    cream
lemon juice to taste
salt and white pepper
few chervil leaves

Note: *Add the scallops at
the last possible moment
and don't boil them as they
toughen with cooking.*

*From being rare items in the smarter fish shops,
scallops have become widely available and now
appear on many supermarket slabs. This way of
using them makes a pale, creamy and sophisticated
soup, which is very elegant at the start of a formal
dinner party.*

Melt the butter in a saucepan. Add the flour
and cook over a gentle heat, stirring
constantly for about 2 minutes without
browning. Gradually pour on the stock and
milk, and whisk until the soup has thickened.
Add the double cream and simmer gently for
20 minutes, stirring occasionally to ensure that
the soup doesn't stick to the pan.

Meanwhile, soak the scallops in cold water
for 2−3 minutes, lift them out and drain them,
checking each one for sand. Remove the corals
and set aside. Carefully trim the scallop whites
(it is vital that all the chewy bits are removed
or the smooth effect will be ruined) and cut
them into large slices. Put them into a bowl,
cover with clingfilm and refrigerate until ready
to use.

Take the soup off the heat and allow it to
cool before adding the corals. Blend in a
liquidizer until smooth, then season and add
the lemon juice. Return the soup to the
saucepan, add the scallop whites and continue
to cook for 1−2 minutes. Check seasoning and
decorate with a few chervil leaves before
serving.

Advance preparation: You can cook the
soup up to adding the corals, but don't add the
scallop whites until reheating
Preparation and cooking time: 35 minutes

COURGETTE AND CAULIFLOWER SOUP

Serves 6

1 × 675 g (1½ lb) cauliflower
1.75 litres (3 pints) water
225 g (½ lb) courgettes
salt and white pepper
1 sprig of basil

This simple soup looks very pretty with its green garnish of strips of courgette skin and chopped fresh basil. Serve it with black bread for even more colour contrast.

Cut the cauliflower into florets. Bring the water to a boil, add the cauliflower florets and cook for 10 minutes. Meanwhile, peel the courgettes and cut the skin into thin strips. Dice the courgette flesh and add to the cauliflower. Cook for a further 5 minutes, or until tender.

While the vegetables are cooking, blanch the strips of courgette skin in boiling water for 1 minute. Drain and refresh under cold running water. Set aside.

Pour the cauliflower mixture into a blender and process until smooth. Season. Reheat if serving hot. Just before serving, add the courgette strips and the finely chopped basil to the soup.

Advance preparation: The soup can be made several hours ahead of serving, but add the courgette strips and basil at the last minute.
Preparation time: 10 minutes
Cooking time: 15 minutes

CHILLED LETTUCE SOUP

Serves 6

2 large round lettuces
1 bunch spring onions
450 g (1 lb) low-fat natural yoghurt
300 ml (½ pint) whipping cream
1 tablespoon green peppercorns
salt
2 tablespoons finely chopped dill
milk, if desired
1 head chicory

Serve this fresh-tasting chilled soup when the weather is warm – its blend of cool vegetables, yoghurt and cream, lightly spiced with green peppercorns, is very refreshing.

Wash the lettuces and cut off the bases. In a food processor, finely chop the lettuces and spring onions. Add the yoghurt and blend, then add the cream and blend again.

Crush the peppercorns with a pestle and mortar and add them to the soup with salt to taste and the chopped dill. Chill until ready

to serve. If the soup is too thick, add a little milk. Serve in individual bowls with a little finely sliced chicory on top.

Advance preparation: The soup can be made several hours ahead of serving. Stir it well before ladling into bowls.
Preparation time: 5 minutes plus chilling

RED PEPPER SOUP

Serves 6

450 g (1 lb) potatoes, peeled and quartered
4 × 150 g (5 oz) jars roasted red peppers (pimientos), drained
1 × 400 g (14 oz) tin Italian peeled tomatoes
150 ml (¼ pint) sour cream
salt and black pepper
6 tablespoons diced cucumber

The flavour of this cool, creamy soup is delightful, and crisp breadsticks would make a good accompaniment. For a lower-fat version which tastes equally delicious, you could substitute Greek-style yoghurt for the sour cream.

Put the potatoes in a saucepan of cold water, bring to the boil and boil for 20 minutes or until soft. Drain the potatoes, but retain the water. In a food processor, process the drained red peppers with the potatoes until smooth. Do not over-blend as this will cause the potatoes to become gluey.

Add the tin of tomatoes and enough potato water to make the mixture up to

1 litre (1¾ pints). Blend well until smooth. Add the sour cream and season to taste. Leave to cool. Serve at room temperature, garnished with diced cucumber.

Preparation time: 15 minutes plus cooling
Cooking time: 20 minutes

SPINACH AND PASTA SOUP

Serves 6

675 g (1½ lb) fresh spinach, or
    2 × 275 g (10 oz) packets
    frozen spinach, defrosted
2 tablespoons olive oil
1 bunch spring onions, finely
    sliced
1.4 litres (2½ pints) water
1 round lettuce, shredded
340 g (¾ lb) potatoes, peeled
    and diced
salt and black pepper
50 g (2 oz) soup pasta
2 tablespoons grated
    Parmesan cheese
Parmesan cheese to serve
1 jar pesto sauce to serve

This substantial soup is a beautiful dark green colour, and it smells wonderful too, with the addition of the Italian basil sauce, pesto. Serve the soup as a starter before a light main course, or for lunch with some crusty bread.

If using fresh spinach, remove the ribs and wash the leaves several times in cold water. Or squeeze excess water from frozen spinach. Heat the olive oil in a saucepan and cook the spring onions for 3–4 minutes, or until tender. Add the water and the lettuce, potatoes and three-quarters of the spinach. Season. Bring to a boil, then cover and simmer for 20 minutes.

Bring the soup back to a full boil and add the pasta and Parmesan cheese. Cook for 4–6 minutes, or until the pasta is almost cooked. Add the remaining spinach, stir well and cook until the pasta is *al dente*. Check the seasoning.

Serve immediately with bowls of grated Parmesan cheese and pesto sauce.

Preparation time: 20 minutes
Cooking time: 35–40 minutes

SPICY VEGETABLE SOUP

Serves 6

40 g (1½ oz) butter
2 onions, coarsely chopped
2 cloves garlic, chopped
2 medium carrots, finely
    chopped
675 g (1½ lb) yellow
    courgettes
    or custard marrow
450 g (1 lb) potatoes
600 ml (1 pint) chicken stock
2 teaspoons lemon juice
¼ teaspoon powdered
    mustard
salt and white pepper
tabasco sauce to taste
1 × 225 g (8 oz) tin sweetcorn
1 tablespoon chopped chives
4–6 tablespoons salsa or
    bottled taco sauce

Vegetable soup with a difference! The colourful mixture of vegetables is enlivened with a little hot mustard and tabasco sauce, just enough to perk up the flavours.

Melt the butter in a large saucepan, add the onions, garlic and carrots and cook for 5 minutes, or until the onions are tender. Peel and chop the yellow courgettes or custard marrow, and the potatoes. Add the courgettes or custard marrow, potatoes, 450 ml (¾ pint) of the chicken stock, the lemon juice, mustard, and pepper and tabasco sauce to taste to the saucepan. Bring to a boil and simmer, covered, for 10 minutes, or until all the vegetables are soft.

Allow to cool slightly.

Process the soup in a blender until smooth, in batches, and transfer to a clean pan. Add the remaining chicken stock, and the sweetcorn. Simmer for a further 5 minutes. Transfer to a serving tureen and garnish with chopped chives. Serve immediately, and let each guest add the salsa or taco sauce.

Advance preparation: The soup can be made the day before and then reheated and garnished just before serving.
Preparation time: 25 minutes
Cooking time: 25 minutes

GARLIC SOUP

Serves 6

2 heads garlic
450 g (1 lb) potatoes
1.5 litres (2½ pints) vegetable
    stock
2 tablespoons olive oil
1 sprig thyme
1 sprig parsley
2 tablespoons finely grated
    Parmesan cheese
salt and black pepper
6 tablespoons grated Cheddar
    cheese
6 slices of French bread

Two heads of garlic may seem a lot, but cooked this way, the garlic is very mild, with a subtle sweet flavour. Cheese-topped croûtons garnish each serving of this delicious soup.

Separate the heads of garlic into cloves and peel. Peel the potatoes. Place the first six ingredients in a saucepan. Bring just to a boil, then cover and simmer for 1 hour. Heat the grill. Remove the thyme, and process the soup in a blender until smooth. Return to the pan and stir in the Parmesan cheese and seasoning. Keep hot.

Place a tablespoon of Cheddar cheese on each slice of French bread and grill until melted and golden brown. Serve the soup in individual bowls with a grilled cheese croûton in the middle.

Advance preparation: The soup can be made the day before and reheated just before serving, but prepare the cheese croûtons at the last minute.
Preparation time: 25 minutes
Cooking time: 1¼ hours

FISH

STIR-FRIED FISH AND GREEN BEANS

Illustrated on page 78

Serves 4

450 g (1 lb) haddock fillet, or other white fish
120 g (4 oz) green beans
1 clove garlic
3 tablespoons corn oil
3 tablespoons flaked almonds
2 tablespoons soy sauce
4 tablespoons oyster sauce

Once you've prepared the ingredients, this cooks very fast. It's best done in a wok (page 79) but you could use a frying pan. Don't overcook it: it's essential the beans stay crisp. Serve with rice.

Skin the haddock, remove any bones and cut into thin strips about 5 cm (2 in) long. Top and tail the green beans and finely chop the garlic.

Heat the oil in the wok and add the flaked almonds, stirring constantly until they are browned. Put on one side of the wok, or remove completely and set aside if you are worried that they will brown too much. Add the beans and garlic to the wok and cook for several minutes until the beans are just crisp. Add the fish and cook, stirring occasionally, for a minute or two until cooked. Finally, add the soy sauce and oyster sauce with the cooked almonds. Stir the ingredients well, season if necessary and serve at once.

Preparation time: 10 minutes
Cooking time: 5 minutes

GRILLED FISH WITH LIME AND CORIANDER

Serves 6

6 × 175 g (6 oz) thin cod fillets, or other white fish
salt and black pepper
85 g (3 oz) melted butter, or 3–4 tablespoons olive oil
1 tablespoon chopped fresh coriander
3 limes

Note: *If you use cutlets for this recipe, the grilling time will be longer – 5 minutes on each side.*

Grilled fish tends to be the staple diet in our household, and there are few things as tasty, nutritious and quick. Thin steaks or fillets of fish won't need turning during cooking and will take 4–5 minutes. Alternatively you could bake the fish in the oven, but don't let it dry out. The lime and coriander gives an exotic flavour, though good old parsley and lemon juice or mustard and orange juice are just as delicious, and now that so many supermarkets are stocking fresh herbs you could experiment with all sorts of other combinations. Dill is a favourite of mine, for instance, and looks so very pretty and feathery as well as tasting marvellous with fish.

Brush the fish with a little melted butter or olive oil and season with salt and black pepper. Grill under a moderate heat for about 5 minutes, basting during cooking to prevent the fish from drying out. The fish is cooked when the flesh flakes with a fork.

While the fish is cooking, mix the coriander with the juice of two limes. Transfer the fish to serving plates and spoon over the lime and coriander dressing. Cut the remaining lime into slices and decorate each piece of fish with a lime twist.

Preparation and cooking time: 10 minutes

BAKED FISH WITH TARRAGON

Illustrated on page 77

Serves 6

900 g (2 lb) cod fillets, or other white fish
1 × 275 g (10 oz) tin sliced mushrooms
600 ml (1 pint) natural yoghurt
6 tablespoons mayonnaise
1 tablespoon lemon juice
2 teaspoons dried tarragon
salt and black pepper
parsley to garnish

Note: *Add a little cornflour to the yoghurt and mayonnaise sauce before pouring over the fish to prevent curdling.*

This is a simple and delicious fish recipe and there are endless variations you could experiment with such as using a teaspoon of curry powder instead of the tarragon, or adding grapes to give it a 'Véronique' look. Its great advantage is that it can easily be prepared ahead of time and then stuck in the oven for 25 minutes while you get on with something else.

Heat the oven to 350°F (180°C, gas mark 4). Skin and bone the fish and place it in the base of a gratin dish, with the sliced mushrooms on top. Mix the yoghurt, mayonnaise, lemon juice and dried tarragon together in a bowl, season with salt and black pepper and pour the sauce over the fish and mushrooms. Cover with foil and bake in the preheated oven for 25 minutes or until the fish flakes with a fork. Serve immediately, garnished with parsley.

Preparation time: 10 minutes
Cooking time: 25 minutes

FISH EN CROÛTE

Illustrated on page 25

Serves 6

900 g (2 lb) haddock fillet, or other white fish
725 g (1 lb 10 oz) frozen chopped spinach
a pinch of mace
salt and black pepper
900 g (2 lb) puff pastry
flour for dusting
1 beaten egg for glazing

Note: *As the scales form an extra layer, the second fish layer must not be too thick or it will not cook through.*
The dish is best served straight from the oven, so put it in 10 minutes before your guests arrive. Turn it down to 325°F (160°C, gas mark 3) just before you go into dinner, so that it stays warm while you eat the first course.

This looks magnificent and is much easier than you would think; use bought puff pastry. You could improvise the 'scales' with a bottle top or simply score the pastry with a knife.

Heat the oven to 400°F (200°C, gas mark 6). Defrost the spinach over a low heat, then place it in a sieve and squeeze out all the excess moisture. Transfer to a bowl and season well with mace, salt and black pepper.

Sprinkle the work surface with a little flour and roll out half the pastry. Cut a fish shape from the pastry, large enough to take one side of the fish. Sprinkle a baking sheet with water, place the pastry fish on it and brush the edges of the pastry with egg glaze. Roll out the other half of the pastry so that it is thinner than the first layer, and cut out another fish shape at least 3.8 cm (1½ in) larger than the first as it has to cover the filling. Place half the haddock in the centre of the pastry and season. Spread the spinach evenly over the top, place the rest of the haddock fillets on the spinach and cover with the second pastry fish. Trim the pastry as necessary. Brush off any excess flour and glaze with egg.

To make the 'scales' cut out crescents from the pastry trimmings with a small cutter. Place the scales on the fish, starting from the tail. Cut two circles 2.5 cm (1 in) and 1.9 cm (¾ in) in diameter and position for the eye. Brush the pastry scales with egg glaze. With a sharp knife make three incisions in the pastry so the steam can escape. Cook the fish in the preheated oven for 40 minutes, or until the pastry is puffed and golden brown. Check the fish during cooking as the head and tail may need to be covered with foil; they tend to cook faster than the centre. When cooked, transfer to a serving dish and serve with a Watercress sauce (page 139).

Advance preparation: The dish can be prepared about 2 hours in advance, but not much more, as the pastry and fish should be refrigerated before cooking. However, some fridges are not large enough to accommodate baking trays, so you will have to find a cool place for the pastry fish until you are ready to cook it.
Preparation time: 40 minutes
Cooking time: 40 minutes

TRICOLOUR FISH MOUSSE

Illustrated on page 31

Serves 6

450 g (1 lb) haddock fillets
225 g (½ lb) smoked salmon
120 g (4 oz) frozen chopped spinach, defrosted and cooked
600 ml (1 pint) milk
4 sprigs tarragon
450 ml (¾ pint) double cream
salt and black pepper
200 g (7 oz) cream cheese
150 ml (¼ pint) chicken stock
1 tablespoon lemon juice
2 × 15 g (½ oz) packet powdered gelatine
watercress to garnish

A spectacular, triple-layered mousse of pink, green and white, this creates a wonderful centrepiece for a summer buffet. For less formal occasions, omit the salmon and just use haddock and spinach.

Remove the skin and bones from the haddock and place it in a flameproof gratin dish with half the milk and the tarragon sprigs. Simmer for 15 minutes or until the fish flakes with a fork. When it is cooked, remove the tarragon and transfer the fish and liquid to a blender. Blend until smooth, then add 300 ml (½ pint) of the cream and blend again. Add salt and place in the fridge.

Chop the smoked salmon, add the cream cheese and blend. Gradually add the stock and the rest of the milk and double cream. Add lemon juice and seasoning to taste.

Next dissolve 2 teaspoons of gelatine in water according to the manufacturer's instructions. Mix this into the salmon mixture.

Wet the base of a 1.4 litre (2½ pint) fish mould or ring mould, pour the salmon mousse into it and refrigerate until set. Dissolve the remaining gelatine in 5 tablespoons of water. Remove the haddock mixture from the fridge and combine it with the gelatine, then split the mixture in two and place one half in the fridge. When the salmon mousse has set (about 15 minutes), pour one batch of haddock mousse on top and return to the fridge for 15 – 20 minutes. Meanwhile add the cold cooked spinach to the remaining haddock batch. Pour it onto the set salmon and haddock mixture in the mould and leave to set for 2 hours.

To serve, release the edges of the mousse with a knife, dip the base of the mould into warm water and gently turn the mousse out onto a serving dish. Garnish with watercress.

Preparation and cooking time: 50 minutes
Setting time: 3 hours

TUNA FISH CAKES

Illustrated on page 39

Makes 6 or 12

2 × 225 g (8 oz) tin tuna
fish
450 g (1 lb) potatoes
30 g (1 oz) butter
1 egg, beaten
a little horseradish
(optional)
salt and black pepper
fresh or packet natural
breadcrumbs for coating
3 tablespoons corn oil

Note: *If the breadcrumbs
don't stick to the fish cakes,
coat them with beaten egg
before rolling.*

I've always loved fish cakes, and this version using a tin of tuna from the store cupboard is absolutely delicious and very easy. You could cheat even more and use instant mashed potato for speed but the taste won't be quite the same. They can be kept warm for up to an hour without spoiling, so they make ideal brunch food, but use them for any casual occasion when your guests may be arriving and eating at staggered times.

Peel and coarsely chop the potatoes, place them in a saucepan of cold water, bring to a boil and cook until soft – about 15 minutes. Drain and mash the potatoes with the butter. Drain the tuna fish, flake it with a fork and add it to the potatoes. Mix the ingredients well and add the beaten egg, and horseradish if using, then season with salt and pepper and mix again.

Place the breadcrumbs on a flat dish or tray. Form the fish and potato mixture into cakes and roll them in the breadcrumbs until they are well covered. The mixture will make 6 large fish cakes, or 12 small ones for children or as a picnic snack.

Heat the oil in a frying pan and, when it is hot, cook the fish cakes for a few minutes on each side to crisp the outside and heat the inside. Remove from the pan, drain on kitchen paper and serve.

Preparation and cooking time: 40 minutes

PAELLA

Illustrated on page 17

Serves 10

10 chicken drumsticks
450 g (1 lb) bacon, cut into
strips
450 g (1 lb) squid, cleaned
and cut into rings
450 g (1 lb) chorizo, thinly
sliced
675 g (1½ lb) tomatoes,
peeled, seeded and cut
into strips
450 g (1 lb) cod or haddock
fillets, cut into strips
450 g (1 lb) unpeeled
shrimps
2 litres (4 lb) mussels,
cleaned
150 ml (¼ pint) olive oil
2 large onions, sliced
1 green pepper, seeded and
sliced
900 g (2 lb) long grain rice
1.1 litre (2 pints) chicken
stock
salt and black pepper

This is a complete meal cooked in one pan – easy on the washing up! For smaller quantities, a large iron frying pan would do in place of a paella pan. The ingredients can be varied according to taste and you'll only need a simple salad to accompany it. If you have any left over, don't reheat it: remove the shells from the mussels and shrimps and the bones from the chicken, and mix with a yoghurt mayonnaise and chopped fresh herbs. Chill and serve on a bed of green salad – it's so delicious it's worth making an extra quantity.

Heat the oil in a paella pan and brown the chicken pieces for 10–12 minutes so that they are partially cooked. Add the onions, green pepper and bacon, and cook until the onions are soft. Add the rice and cook, stirring constantly, for 2–3 minutes or until the rice is transparent and the oil is absorbed. Add the stock, and season with salt and black pepper. Add the remaining ingredients (except the shrimps) with the mussels on top.

Half an hour before serving, bring the paella to a boil over direct heat and cook gently, uncovered, until all the liquid has been absorbed (about 18 minutes) and the rice is cooked. Add more stock if the liquid evaporates before the rice is cooked. Add the shrimps to the paella and cook over a low heat for 5–10 minutes to allow the flavours to blend. Serve immediately, from the pan.

Advance preparation: The paella ingredients can be assembled in advance in the pan and left in a cold place, such as a larder. Don't add the stock until you are cooking the paella as it is dangerous for raw fish to sit in warm stock. If you don't have a larder, leave the prepared fish, chicken and tomatoes in the fridge and add them to the paella pan at the last moment – it will only take a couple of minutes.

Preparation time: 25 minutes
Cooking time: 40 minutes

CRAB AND BLUE CHEESE QUICHE

Serves 4–6

250 g (9 oz) shortcrust pastry
100 g (3½ oz) fresh or frozen and thawed crab meat
100 g (3½ oz) rindless Bresse Bleu, chopped
120 g (4 oz) Cheddar cheese, finely grated
3 eggs (size 2)
300 ml (½ pint) double cream
freshly grated nutmeg
salt and white pepper

The filling for this delicious quiche combines crab meat, Bresse Bleu cheese, Cheddar cheese, eggs and cream. As it is rich, serve the quiche with a crisp, sharply dressed salad.

Roll out the pastry on a lightly floured surface and use to line a 20 cm (8 in) flan dish. Prick the base and chill for 20 minutes. Heat the oven to 350°F (180°C, gas mark 4). Line the pastry case with greaseproof paper and weigh down with dried beans. Bake blind in the preheated oven for 20 minutes, then remove the paper and beans and bake for a further 10 minutes.

Arrange the crab meat, Bresse Bleu and Cheddar in the pastry case. In a bowl, whisk the eggs, cream, nutmeg and seasoning until well mixed. Pour into the pastry case. Bake the quiche in the middle of the preheated oven for 40 minutes, or until the filling is golden and a knife inserted in the middle comes out clean. Allow to cool on a wire rack for 10 minutes before serving.

Preparation time: 35 minutes plus chilling
Cooking time: 1 hour 10 minutes plus cooling

FISH TAGINE WITH TOMATO

Serves 6

1 whole firm-fleshed white fish, weighing about 2.2 kg (5 lb), cleaned, scaled and head removed
3 large potatoes, peeled, parboiled and sliced
charmoula (see page 140)
3 ripe tomatoes, sliced
3 green peppers, seeded and sliced
1–2 cloves garlic, chopped
150 ml (¼ pint) water
2–3 tablespoons lemon juice
1½ tablespoons tomato purée
3 tablespoons vegetable oil

In this Moroccan dish, a whole fish is baked with a topping of sliced potato, tomato and green pepper. The flavour comes from a piquant blend of herbs, spices, garlic and lemon juice, called charmoula (page 140).

Heat the oven to 400°F (200°C, gas mark 6). Lay bamboo skewers, or shortened chopsticks, across the bottom of a baking dish to form a lattice. Place the fish on the sticks. Layer the potato slices around it and sprinkle over some charmoula; layer on the tomato and green pepper, with charmoula in between. Sprinkle on the garlic.

Combine the remaining ingredients and pour over the fish. Cover with foil and bake in the preheated oven for 35 minutes. Raise the oven heat to 425°F (220°C, gas mark 7), remove the foil and bake for a further 20 minutes. Serve warm.

Advance preparation: The charmoula can be made well ahead of time.
Preparation time: 45 minutes
Cooking time: 55 minutes

RED SNAPPER WITH ALMOND PASTE

Serves 6

225 g (½ lb) blanched almonds, toasted
50 g (2 oz) butter, at room temperature
1 tablespoon orange-flower water
1 teaspoon ground cinnamon
15 g (½ oz) icing sugar
7 tablespoons water
1 red snapper, weighing about 1.4 kg (3 lb), cleaned and scaled
2 onions, finely chopped
pinch of saffron powder
black pepper
freshly cooked vegetables, to garnish

For this unusual recipe, a whole fish is stuffed and covered with an exotic spiced almond paste, and then baked on a bed of saffron-coloured onions. Simply prepared green vegetables would make the best accompaniments to complement the subtle flavour of the dish.

Heat the oven to 375°F (190°C, gas mark 5). In a food processor, chop the almonds, then add 40 g (1½ oz) of the butter, the orange-flower water, cinnamon, sugar and 3 tablespoons water and blend to a smooth paste. Be careful not to overwork in the food processor or the mixture will become very oily. Stuff the fish with half the paste.

Rub an ovenproof dish with 10 g (½ oz) butter. Add the onions, remaining water and saffron and mix. Season. Place the fish on top of the bed of onions. Spread the rest of the paste over the fish. Cover with foil and bake in the preheated oven for 30 minutes, then remove the foil and cook for a further 15 minutes, to allow the almond crust to crisp.

Transfer the fish to a serving dish and garnish the sides of the fish with vegetables.

Preparation time: 25 minutes
Cooking time: 45 minutes

PLAICE STUFFED WITH SPINACH

Serves 6

340 g (¾ lb) frozen chopped
   spinach, defrosted
1 egg, beaten
1 egg yolk
7 tablespoons garlic croûtons,
   slightly crushed
85 g (3 oz) Parmesan cheese,
   grated
6 tablespoons soured cream
6 tinned water chestnuts,
   chopped
celery salt
6 fresh plaice or other white
   fish fillets

Here plaice fillets are rolled around a delicious stuffing of spinach, soured cream, Parmesan cheese and crunchy water chestnuts. Serve it either plain or with a fresh tomato sauce.

Heat the oven to 350°F (180°C, gas mark 4). Press out any liquid from the spinach, then put it in a bowl. Add the whole egg, egg yolk, croûtons, cheese, soured cream, water chestnuts and celery salt to taste. Mix together well.

Cut each fish fillet in half lengthways. Spread the stuffing on each piece of fish and roll up. Place the rolls seam down in a baking dish. Bake in the preheated oven for 30 minutes or until the fish flakes easily when tested with a fork.

Preparation time: 30 minutes
Cooking time: 30 minutes

SALMON AND CHEESE CHOWDER

Serves 4

40 g (1½ oz) butter
3 sticks celery, chopped
3 carrots, chopped
85 g (3 oz) plain flour
¼ teaspoon paprika
black pepper
600 ml (1 pint) fish stock
600 ml (1 pint) milk
4 tablespoons dry white wine
400 g (14 oz) salmon fillet
85 g (3 oz) mild Cheddar
   cheese, grated
3 tablespoons chopped dill

Chowders are hearty, filling soups, but they can be elegant too, as this recipe shows. Fresh salmon, vegetables and Cheddar cheese are combined to make this one, with white wine and fresh dill for a special flavour.

Melt the butter in a saucepan and cook the celery and carrot for 5 minutes or until tender, stirring occasionally. Stir in the flour and paprika and season to taste with black pepper. Pour in the fish stock, milk and white wine, stirring constantly, and cook until the soup thickens. Allow to simmer gently for 10 minutes.

Remove any bones and skin from the salmon; flake it into the soup. Continue to cook gently for 5 minutes. Stir in the cheese and cook, until it has melted. Stir in 1 tablespoon chopped dill. Ladle the soup into bowls and sprinkle the remaining dill over the top. Serve immediately.

Preparation time: 15 minutes
Cooking time: 35 minutes

PRAWN SHELLS

Serves 4

225 g (8 oz) frozen spinach,
   defrosted
15 g (½ oz) butter
½ stick celery, chopped
4 spring onions, sliced
85 g (3 oz) Cheddar cheese,
   finely grated
1 egg, beaten
½ teaspoon ground coriander
black pepper
450 g (1 lb) puff pastry
120 g (4 oz) peeled cooked
   prawns
beaten egg to glaze

Scallop shells are used as the moulds for these savoury pastries, giving them a very attractive appearance. The filling is a delicately spiced mixture of prawns, spinach and Cheddar cheese.

Squeeze any excess liquid from the spinach. Melt the butter in a saucepan and cook the celery and spring onions for 5 minutes or until tender, stirring occasionally. Add the spinach and cook to evaporate any excess water. Remove from the heat and add the cheese, egg and coriander. Season with pepper.

Heat the oven to 400°F (200°C, gas mark 6). Roll out the pastry to a 50 × 25 cm (20 × 10 in) rectangle and cut into eight 12.5 cm (5 in) squares. Line each of four buttered scallop shells with a pastry square. Divide the spinach mixture and prawns among the shells. Brush the pastry edges with egg. Cut a hole in the centre of each remaining pastry square and place it on top of the shell. Trim the edges, seal and flute. Use the pastry trimmings to decorate the top. Brush the top with egg.

Arrange the shells on a baking sheet, with crumpled foil around to keep them upright, and bake in the preheated oven for 20–25 minutes.

Preparation time: 30 minutes
Cooking time: 30–35 minutes

EGGS, CHEESE AND PASTA

SOUFFLÉ OMELETTES

Serves 2

4 eggs, separated
2 tablespoons milk or cream
pinch of salt or sugar (for savoury or sweet omelette)
15 g (½ oz) butter
1 tablespoon caster sugar (for sweet omelette)
1 tablespoon Parmesan cheese (for savoury omelette)

This really is simply a showy, puffy omelette which can be filled with a variety of things, sweet or savoury. It's the perfect standby for unexpected guests. Like a soufflé, the omelette must be served immediately.

Combine the egg yolks, milk (or cream) and salt (or sugar) and beat well. Whisk the egg whites until stiff and fold in the egg yolk mixture. Heat the grill to high.

Melt the butter in the omelette pan and, when it is foaming, pour in the egg mixture. Cook over a moderate heat until the underside is golden brown, then place under the preheated grill to brown lightly on top. Add the filling, fold the omelette in half and transfer to a warmed serving dish. Serve sprinkled with caster sugar or Parmesan.

Preparation and cooking time: 12 minutes

Bacon and Mushroom Filling

Illustrated on page 74

3 rashers streaky bacon
120 g (¼ lb) mushrooms
2–3 tablespoons chopped parsley

Remove the bacon rind and cut the rashers into strips across. Fry the bacon in a small frying pan until crispy. Slice and add the mushrooms. Cook for 2–3 minutes until softened. Add the chopped parsley, season and keep warm until ready to use.

Preparation and cooking time: 5 minutes

Shrimp and Chervil Filling

50 g (2 oz) shrimps, defrosted if necessary
15 g (½ oz) butter
2–3 tablespoons chopped chervil

Melt the butter in a pan and add the shrimps. Cook until hot and then add the chopped chervil. Don't overcook the shrimps as they will become tough. Keep the filling warm until ready to use.

Preparation and cooking time: 5 minutes

Tomato and Basil Filling

225 g (½ lb) tomatoes
1 shallot, chopped
30 g (1 oz) butter
2 teaspoons fresh basil or
1 teaspoon dried basil

Peel, seed and chop the tomatoes. Fry the shallot in the butter until transparent. Add the tomato and basil. (If using dried basil, soak in a little lemon juice first.) Season with salt and black pepper, simmer for 10 minutes and keep warm until ready to serve.

Preparation and cooking time: 15 minutes

Banana and Rum Filling

1 banana
15 g (½ oz) butter
1 tablespoon brown sugar
1 tablespoon dark rum

Melt the butter in a pan and fry the sliced banana in it. Add the sugar and rum, heat through and keep warm until ready to use.

Preparation and cooking time: 5 minutes

Strawberry and Redcurrant Filling

85 g (3 oz) strawberries
2 tablespoons redcurrant jelly
1 tablespoon caster sugar
lemon juice to taste

Melt the redcurrant jelly over a low heat. Slice the strawberries, and add to the pan. Sprinkle with sugar and lemon juice to taste. Keep warm until ready to use, but not for too long as the strawberries will go mushy.

Preparation and cooking time: 5 minutes

BASIC ROULADE

Serves 6

50 g (2 oz) butter
50 g (2 oz) flour
300 ml ($\frac{1}{2}$ pint) milk
4 eggs, separated
butter for greasing
flour for coating

Note: *Add 125 g (4 oz) ground almonds to the egg mixture, if you like.*

A roulade is a very showy, light lunch dish or starter. It's quite easy to make and can be served hot or cold, with a variety of fillings. The only slightly tricky bit is peeling off the backing paper: be very careful how you do it.

Heat the oven to 400°F (200°C, gas mark 6). Line a Swiss roll tin 34 × 24 cm (13$\frac{1}{2}$ × 9$\frac{1}{2}$ in) using non-stick baking paper or greaseproof paper, brushed with melted butter and coated lightly with flour.

Melt the butter in a saucepan, add the flour and cook for a couple of minutes. Gradually add the milk and cook for a further 2 minutes. Remove from the heat and add the egg yolks, one at a time, stirring them in. Whisk the egg whites until they are stiff and fold them into the mixture with a large metal spoon, then pour the mixture into the prepared Swiss roll tin and spread it evenly over the base. Bake in the oven for 20 minutes.

Remove the hot roulade from the oven, and turn it out onto a sheet of greaseproof or non-stick paper. With a knife, gently ease the roulade away from the lining paper. If you are serving the roulade warm, spread the filling over the surface, then roll it lengthways, like a Swiss roll. Slide the roulade onto a warmed dish and serve, or keep warm in the oven at 350°F (180°C, gas mark 4) until ready to serve. If serving cold, remove the roulade from the oven, roll it and leave to cool. When it is cold, unroll, spread with the filling and roll up again. Wrap the filled roulade loosely in a clean tea towel and chill in the refrigerator overnight. To serve, cut two slices of the roulade for each person.

Advance preparation: You can reheat the roulade gently for 15 – 20 minutes at 325°F (160°C, gas mark 3), before serving.
Preparation time: 15 minutes
Cooking time: 20 minutes
Assembly time: 10 minutes

SPINACH ROULADE

Serves 6

Illustrated on page 15

225 g (8 oz) spinach, defrosted and chopped
15 g ($\frac{1}{2}$ oz) butter
salt and black pepper
pinch of nutmeg
150 ml ($\frac{1}{4}$ pint) single cream
4 large eggs, separated
Parmesan cheese, to serve

This delicious variation on the basic recipe incorporates spinach into the roulade and doesn't contain flour. I'd recommend it for a first attempt.

Grease and line a 22.5 × 33 cm (10 × 13 in) Swiss roll tin, using non-stick baking paper or oiled greaseproof paper. Heat the oven to 400°F (200°C, gas mark 6). Melt the butter in a thick saucepan, add the drained chopped spinach and stir gently until the moisture has evaporated. Mix in the salt, pepper, nutmeg, cream and egg yolks. In a bowl, whisk the egg whites until stiff, but not dry, and fold them into the spinach mixture. Pour into the tin and bake in the preheated oven for 10 – 15 minutes, until the roulade is firm.

Turn the cooked roulade out onto a sheet of non-stick or greaseproof paper. Peel off the lining paper, spread the filling evenly over the roulade and roll it up again like a Swiss roll. Slide the roulade onto a flat dish, sprinkle with Parmesan and serve.

Preparation time: 10 minutes
Cooking time: 20 minutes
Assembly time: 10 minutes

Tuna Filling

Illustrated on page 29

2 × 225 g ($\frac{1}{2}$ lb) tin tuna fish
175 g (6 oz) cream cheese
1 bunch dill, chopped
150 ml ($\frac{1}{4}$ pint) double cream
1 tablespoon lemon juice
salt, pepper and cayenne
lemon and parsley to garnish

This is best used to fill the basic roulade and served cold. Add a little chopped parsley if you want to make the spiral shape more of an obvious contrast to the tuna mixture.

Strain the tuna fish and blend it with the cream cheese, dill and double cream. Add the lemon juice, season with salt, black pepper and a pinch of cayenne and mix well. Garnish the roulade with lemon and parsley.

Preparation time: 5 minutes

Roquefort Filling

Illustrated on page 73

85 g (3 oz) Roquefort cheese
120 g (4 oz) Mascarpone
   cheese
225 g (½ lb) celeriac
lemon juice
black pepper

Do try this – it's absolutely delicious. Although it's particularly good with the basic roulade mixture, it could be used with either. Spread onto hot or cold roulade.

Mix the Roquefort and Mascarpone together with a fork until blended. Trim and grate the celeriac, sprinkle with a little lemon juice, add to the cheese mixture and blend well.

Preparation time: 8 minutes

Ricotta Filling

225 g (8 oz) ricotta or
   2 × 70 g (2¾ oz) packets
   boursin
2 tablespoons yoghurt
2 tablespoons chopped
   chives
2 tablespoons chopped
   parsley

I think this one really complements the spinach roulade: it's tangy and herby and the creamy whiteness looks great against the green roulade.

Beat the ricotta (or boursin) with the yoghurt and herbs and set aside until ready to use.

Preparation time: 5 minutes

Curried Prawn Filling

450 g (1 lb) frozen shelled
   prawns, defrosted
50 g (2 oz) ghee
3 tablespoons biryani paste
2 tablespoons garam masala
6 tablespoons mayonnaise

One really special teaming for the spinach roulade: it's a truly dynamic duo. But do try it with the basic roulade recipe too.

Melt the ghee and stir in the biryani paste and garam masala. Stir briefly to blend and add in the prawns. Cook gently for 5 – 8 minutes, stirring, then leave to stand in the marinade overnight. Drain the prawns and mix with the mayonnaise.

Preparation and cooking time: 10 minutes
Marinating time: 8 hours or overnight

SEAFOOD LASAGNE

Illustrated on page 40

Serves 6

900 g (2 lb) smoked cod or
   haddock fillets
225 g (½ lb) frozen shelled
   prawns, defrosted
2 × 400 g (14 oz) tin lobster
   bisque
12 sheets green no-cook
   lasagne
lemon juice
salt and black pepper
3–4 tablespoons Parmesan
   cheese

Some short cuts are immensely worthwhile, and using 'no-cook' lasagne and a tin of lobster bisque cuts down preparation time dramatically without losing flavour. Serve immediately, and it will taste delicious and creamy.

Heat the oven to 350°F (180°C, gas mark 4). Remove any skin from the fish fillets and cut the fish into 3.8 cm (1½ in) strips. Heat the lobster soup to a pouring consistency and add the lemon juice to taste. Season with salt and pepper.
   Pour a layer of sauce on the base of a rectangular ovenproof dish and add a layer of fish and prawns. Place a layer of lasagne on top. Repeat the layers, finishing with a layer of fish and sauce. Sprinkle on Parmesan cheese.

Cook in the preheated oven for half an hour and serve immediately.

Preparation time: 15 minutes
Cooking time: 30 minutes

PASTA WITH CREAM AND HAM

Illustrated on page 74

Serves 6

575 g (1¼ lb) fresh tagliatelle
    or thin dried
    pasta, such as tonnarelli
300 ml (½ pint) single cream
2 eggs
4 slices ham, chopped
salt and black pepper
Parmesan cheese, to serve

This is a quick pasta dish. The combination of cheese and ham never fails; vary the type and quantity according to what you have.

Cook the pasta in plenty of boiling salted water until *al dente* – approximately 6–8 minutes if fresh, 10–12 minutes if dried.
    Combine the cream and eggs in a bowl.

Strain the pasta and return it to the pan. Pour in the cream and egg mixture and stir well. Add the ham and seasoning. Stir over a very gentle heat for a couple of minutes and serve at once, with a bowl of Parmesan cheese.

Preparation time: 5 minutes
Cooking time: 20 minutes

PASTA AND NUT SALAD

Illustrated on page 31

Serves 6

340 g (12 oz) pasta bows
    (farfalle)
2 tablespoons sunflower oil
50 g (2 oz) pine kernels
50 g (2 oz) shelled walnuts
1 clove garlic
3 tablespoons olive oil
2 tablespoons lemon juice
4 tablespoons chopped
    parsley, or any other fresh
    herbs
1 bunch watercress
salt and black pepper

Pasta salads are becoming increasingly popular, and if you use shapes like bows, spirals and shells it is easy to eat – long strings of spaghetti can be fairly tricky! It makes a good side salad, or is very good on its own, mixed with a little chopped smoked ham.

Preheat the oven to 400°F (200°C, gas mark 6) and toast the pine kernels on a baking tray for 10 minutes. Meanwhile cook the pasta in boiling salted water until it is just *al dente*.

Drain and refresh under cold water, then drain again thoroughly. Toss the pasta in the sunflower oil and set aside.
    Reserve 1 tablespoon of pine kernels, and put the rest, with the remaining ingredients, into a food processor or blender. Blend until the mixture forms a smooth purée, then combine this with the pasta. Sprinkle over the remaining pine kernels and serve.

Preparation and cooking time: 20 minutes

PASTA AND SALAMI SALAD

Serves 6

450 g (1 lb) fusilli
120 g (¼ lb) Napoli salami
120 g (¼ lb) Milano salami
2 cloves garlic
150 ml (¼ pint) olive oil
3 tablespoons mustard
2–3 tablespoons Parmesan
2 tablespoons red wine
    vinegar
salt and black pepper
425 g (15 oz) tin pitted
    black olives

As with the other pasta salad, make sure you buy suitable shapes for easy eating. If you can get the three colours (white, green and orange) – and many supermarkets now sell a good selection of fresh pasta – so much the better: they do look very pretty together. If you don't like the strong taste of salami, prosciutto would also be delicious.

Cook the pasta for 8 minutes, if fresh (10–12 if dried) in boiling salted water. Drain and refresh under cold running water, then dress

with a tablespoon of oil to prevent the pasta sticking together. Remove the skin from the salamis and cut into 1 cm (¼–½ in) cubes. Finely chop the garlic, then add the salami and garlic pieces to the pasta, with the remaining olive oil. Mix well and add the mustard, Parmesan cheese and red wine vinegar. Mix again. Season before adding the pitted black olives and serve.

Preparation and cooking time: 25 minutes

FOUR CHEESE PASTA

Serves 6

575 g (1¼ lb) fresh pasta
50 g (2 oz) each Gruyère,
    Bel Paese and Dolcelatte,
    diced
50 g (2 oz) Parmesan,
    grated
2 tablespoons olive oil
1 clove garlic, crushed
150 ml (¼ pint) single cream
salt and black pepper

This is one of my favourites: the melted cheese perfectly complements the pasta and makes it wonderfully creamy. Use any cheeses as long as they roughly correspond to the types given here. As it is very rich, follow it with a sharply dressed green salad.

Heat the oil in an ovenproof casserole, add the garlic and remove the dish from the heat.

Preheat the oven to 425°F (220°C, gas mark 7). Cook the pasta in boiling salted water for about 8 minutes or until it is *al dente*. Drain and toss in the garlic oil. Add the cream, cheeses, and seasoning and mix well. Place in the oven just long enough for the cheeses to melt.

Preparation and cooking time: 15 minutes

SPAGHETTI WITH WILD MUSHROOMS AND SUN-DRIED TOMATOES

Serves 6 as a starter, 4 as a main course

15 g (½ oz) dried cèpes or
   porcini
1 tablespoon olive oil
2 large onions, chopped
120 g (4 oz) sliced Parma ham
1 teaspoon dried oregano
50 g (2 oz) sun-dried tomatoes,
   sliced
3 cloves garlic, chopped
black pepper
450 g (1 lb) fresh thin spaghetti
4 tablespoons finely grated
   Parmesan cheese
6 tablespoons finely chopped
   fresh coriander

This pasta sauce is rich in flavour – dried wild mushrooms, Parma ham, sun-dried tomatoes and garlic – and fresh coriander makes it that little bit different.

Soak the mushrooms in cold water for 30 minutes. Meanwhile, heat the oil in a frying pan, add the onions, chopped Parma ham, oregano, sun-dried tomatoes, garlic and pepper to taste, and cook for 2–3 minutes, stirring occasionally. Drain the mushrooms, dry them on paper towels and add to the frying pan. Cook, stirring, for 5 minutes longer.

Cook the pasta in boiling water for 3 minutes or until *al dente*. Drain the pasta and place in a serving dish. Pour on the sauce and mix well. Toss in the Parmesan cheese and finely chopped coriander, and serve immediately.

Preparation time: 10 minutes
Cooking time: 10 minutes

RIGATONI WITH GRILLED ASPARAGUS AND PEPPERS

Serves 6 as a starter, 4 as a main course

450 g (1 lb) rigatoni
3 red peppers
12 spears asparagus
4 tablespoons olive oil
2 onions, finely chopped
3 cloves garlic, chopped
120 g (¼ lb) mushrooms,
   sliced
1 teaspoon dried oregano
black pepper
6 tablespoons finely chopped
   parsley
2–3 tablespoons Pecorino
   cheese, finely grated
2–3 tablespoons Parmesan
   cheese, finely grated
50 g (2 oz) pine kernels

For this wonderful dish, the pasta is dressed with a sauce of sweet red peppers, fresh asparagus and mushrooms as well as Parmesan and Pecorino cheeses and pine kernels.

Heat the grill. Grill the red peppers as described on page 85. At the same time, grill the asparagus, brushing the spears with oil so they do not dry out. They will take about 5 minutes. Remove the asparagus and red peppers when ready. Skin the red peppers as described on page 85. Allow the asparagus to cool a little, then remove the skin, cut into 5 cm (2 in) lengths and remove the ends.

Heat the oil in a frying pan and cook the onions and garlic for 5 minutes. Add the mushrooms and cook for 2–3 minutes longer or until softened. Chop the red peppers, discarding the cores and seeds, and add them to the onion mixture, together with the asparagus and herbs. Cook for 2 minutes.

Meanwhile, cook the pasta in boiling water for 3 minutes, or until *al dente*. Drain and transfer to a serving bowl. Pour over the sauce and sprinkle over the cheeses, pine kernels, parsley and seasoning. Toss well together and serve.

Preparation time: 20 minutes
Cooking time: 20 minutes

ORIENTAL NOODLES WITH SESAME

Serves 6

225 g (½ lb) soba noodles
6 cloves garlic
3 tablespoons fresh coriander
4 spring onions, chopped
1–2 teaspoons sesame seeds,
   toasted
175 g (6 oz) smooth peanut
   butter
150 ml (¼ pint) tinned chicken
   consommé or chicken stock
6 tablespoons cider vinegar
3 tablespoons sesame oil
1–2 teaspoons caster sugar
3 tablespoons soy sauce

Try this as part of an oriental feast. The unusual Japanese buckwheat noodles can be bought in shops selling Japanese foods and in some health-food shops.

Put the noodles in a large heatproof bowl, cover with boiling water and leave to soak, stirring occasionally, for 5 minutes, or until they are *al dente*. Drain the noodles in a colander and rinse them under cold running water. Pat the noodles dry and transfer them to a serving bowl.

In a food processor, finely chop the garlic. Add the coriander and process until well mixed. Reserving some of the chopped spring onions and sesame seeds as a garnish, add the remainder to the food processor with the peanut butter, consommé, vinegar, oil, sugar and soy sauce and process until smooth. Pour this sauce over the noodles and toss well. Serve cold with the reserved garnish.

Preparation time: 15–20 minutes

APPLE AND CHEDDAR GRATIN

Serves 6

900 g (2 lb) Granny Smith
　　apples
4 tablespoons lemon juice
½ teaspoon ground cinnamon
1 head celery, sliced
85 g (3 oz) dark brown sugar
50 g (2 oz) plain flour
pinch of salt
50 g (2 oz) cold butter, diced
175 g (6 oz) Cheddar cheese,
　　finely grated

*Here's an apple crumble with a difference – with
the addition of celery to the apples and Cheddar
cheese to the topping, it becomes a satisfying
savoury dish, ideal for lunch or supper.*

Heat the oven to 350°F (180°C, gas mark 4).
Peel, core and slice the apples. Toss the
apple slices with the lemon juice and then
sprinkle over the cinnamon. Arrange the
apple slices in a well-buttered shallow
baking dish and cover with the celery.

Combine the sugar, flour and salt in a
mixing bowl. Rub in the butter until the
mixture resembles coarse breadcrumbs. Mix
in the grated cheese. Sprinkle the cheese
mixture over the apples and celery to cover
evenly. Bake in the preheated oven for 30
minutes, or until the apples are tender.
Serve hot.

Preparation time: 45 minutes
Cooking time: 30 minutes

BRIE PUDDING

Serves 6

16 slices white bread, buttered
225 g (½ lb) Brie, sliced
120 g (¼ lb) Stilton, diced
4 spring onions, chopped
5 large eggs, lightly beaten
1 tablespoon Dijon mustard
600 ml (1 pint) milk
pinch of cayenne pepper
5 tablespoons fresh
　　breadcrumbs
4 tablespoons grated
　　Parmesan cheese
30 g (1 oz) unsalted butter

*This savoury bread pudding combines Brie and
Stilton cheeses with a mustard-flavoured custard
and has a crisp crumb and Parmesan topping.
Serve it with a tomato and onion salad or a green
salad dressed with a sesame oil vinaigrette.*

Remove the crusts from the bread. Layer the
bread, the Brie and Stilton cheeses and the
spring onions in a greased shallow baking
dish. In a bowl, whisk the eggs with the
mustard, add the milk and cayenne and
whisk again. Pour the egg mixture slowly
into the baking dish, then leave to stand for
30 minutes.

Heat the oven to 350°F (180°C, gas mark
4). In a small bowl, combine the
breadcrumbs and Parmesan cheese.
Sprinkle evenly over the pudding and dot it
with butter. Bake the pudding in the
preheated oven for 50–60 minutes or until it
is puffed and golden. Serve hot.

Preparation time: 50 minutes
Cooking time: 50–60 minutes

EGGS IN CHEESE SAUCE

Serves 6

40 g (1½ oz) butter
3 tablespoons plain flour
300–450 ml (½–¾ pint) milk
salt and black pepper
120 g (4 oz) Cheddar cheese,
　　grated
6 large eggs
3 wholemeal rolls, halved

*What could be better for lunch or supper than
eggs baked in a lovely cheesy sauce, served on
wholemeal rolls. This is such a simple dish and yet
it is so satisfying.*

Heat the oven to 350°F (180°C, gas mark 4).
To make the sauce, melt the butter in a
saucepan, add the flour, whisking
constantly, and cook for 3 minutes.
Gradually stir in the milk and cook, stirring,
until the sauce is thick and smooth. Leave to
simmer for 5 minutes.
　　Season the sauce and add half the cheese.
Pour half of the sauce into a 20 cm (8 in)
square ovenproof dish. Carefully break the
eggs into the sauce and cover with the rest of
the sauce. Sprinkle over the remaining
cheese.

Bake in the preheated oven for 15–20
minutes or until the eggs are cooked and the
surface is golden brown. Serve
immediately, placing each egg on half a
wholemeal roll.

Preparation time: 10 minutes
Cooking time: 25–30 minutes

CHICKEN AND BLACK OLIVE CASSEROLE

Illustrated on page 48

Serves 6

6 portions of chicken
2 tablespoons oil
3 small onions, sliced
40 g (1½ oz) butter
40 g (1½ oz) flour
450 ml (¾ pint) hot chicken
    stock
150 ml (¼ pint) dry red wine
1 bay leaf
340 g (¾ lb) mushrooms
salt and black pepper
half a 400 g (14 oz) can
    black pitted olives

Many chicken dishes tend to look bland: this rich, dark one makes a welcome change. You can leave out the olives or substitute prunes or capers.

Heat the oven to 375°F (190°C, gas mark 5). Remove the skin from the chicken pieces and put them aside. Heat the oil in a frying pan and fry the onions for 10 minutes. Melt the butter in a flameproof casserole, add the flour and stir constantly to form a roux. Gradually add 300 ml (½ pint) chicken stock, the red wine and bay leaf, stirring constantly. Bring to a boil, reduce the heat and simmer for 10 minutes.

    Clean and slice the mushrooms and add them to the onions. Continue to cook for 5 minutes, or until the onions are browned and the mushrooms are soft. Season the sauce, add the chicken pieces and the onion and mushroom mixture. Pour the remaining chicken stock into the frying pan, stirring well with a wooden spoon. When it is heated through, pour it into the casserole, mix well, cover and cook in the oven for 40 minutes. Add the drained olives and cook for 20 minutes or until the chicken is tender.

Advance preparation: The casserole can be cooked the day before, but remove and store in a cool place after 40 minutes in the oven. Add the olives when reheating.
Preparation time: 25 minutes
Cooking time: 1 hour

Pie Variation

340 g (12 oz) shortcrust
    pastry
2 litres (3–3½ pints) pie dish
1 beaten egg for glazing
chicken casseroie filling
    (see above), cooked for
    only 30 minutes

Roll out the pastry to 0.6–1.2 cm (¼–½ in) thick, and 5 cm (2 in) larger than the pie dish. Cut a strip of pastry 2.5 cm (1 in) wide. Brush the rim of the dish with the beaten egg, line it with the pastry strip, and brush this with the beaten egg too. Add the chicken casserole filling and set a pie funnel in the centre. Place the remaining pastry over the casserole, seal it, knock up the edges, and make a hole in the centre to allow steam to escape. Decorate as desired and refrigerate the pie until ready to cook. Cook in a preheated oven at 375°F (190°C, gas mark 5) for 25–30 minutes.

Preparation time: 10 minutes
Cooking time: 25–30 minutes

CHICKEN IN WALNUT SAUCE

Illustrated on page 61

Serves 6

1 × 1.4 kg (3 lb) chicken
1 large onion, chopped
2 sticks celery, chopped
9 peppercorns
½ bunch of parsley
1 bay leaf
50 g (2 oz) walnuts
2 cloves garlic
50 g (2 oz) cream cheese
150 ml (¼ pint) double
    cream
½ tablespoon red wine
    vinegar
1 drop tabasco
75 ml (3 fl oz) olive oil
salt and black pepper
fresh dill to garnish

This delicious alternative to coronation chicken would be marvellous on a picnic. For extra speed you could even make it with ready-cooked chicken.

Put the chicken into a large saucepan, cover with water and bring to a boil. Remove any scum with a large metal spoon, then add the chopped onion and celery, peppercorns, parsley and bay leaf and simmer for 1½ hours, or until the chicken is so tender that the flesh falls off the bone. Allow the chicken to cool in the stock.

    Meanwhile, chop the walnuts with the garlic cloves. Add the cream cheese and blend. Add the double cream and blend again but do not blend too much or it will curdle; the mixture will look slightly lumpy at this stage because of the walnuts. Add the red wine vinegar and tabasco and, as you pour in the oil, blend together and season to taste. At this stage the mixture will be creamy and almost smooth.

    Drain the chicken, reserving the stock for use in soups or gravies. Remove the chicken flesh from the bone, skin it, cut into slices and fold into the sauce. Place on a serving dish and garnish with fresh dill.

Advance preparation: The chicken can be cooked the day before and stored in a cool place. If the walnut sauce is made the day before, it will solidify in the fridge, so take it out 1–1½ hours before you want to assemble the dish to allow it to come to room temperature.
Preparation time: 10 minutes
Cooking time: 1½ hours

CHICKEN FILO PIE

Illustrated on page 24

Serves 6

1 × 1.4 kg (3 lb) cooked
  chicken
6 sheets filo pastry (see
  page 88)
175 g (6 oz) cream cheese
150 ml (¼ pint) double
  cream
salt and black pepper
1 × 275 g (10 oz) tin sliced
  mushrooms
22.8 cm (9 in) cake tin,
  loose-bottomed
120–175 g (4–6 oz) butter

Note: *The sides of the cake
tin will be hot. So to avoid
burning your hands as you
remove it, place the tin on
something that is higher and
narrower in circumference.
The base of the tin will
balance on top as the sides
of the tin drop down.*

This is a magnificent and very simple pie, and it looks very special as the centrepiece of a formal dinner. You could, of course, cook your own chicken and use fresh button mushrooms (¾ lb) but it isn't necessary if you're in a hurry. It's also very good cold, and whether hot or cold you won't need potatoes — a couple of good vegetables or salad would be more suitable.

Heat the oven to 350°F (180°C, gas mark 4). Remove the meat from the chicken carcass and shred it. In a food processor or blender, mix the cream cheese and double cream, and season with salt and black pepper. Combine the shredded chicken, drained mushrooms and cream cheese mixture and mix well.

Brush a loose-bottomed 22.8 cm (9 in) diameter cake tin with butter. Brush five sheets of filo pastry with plenty of butter and line the cake tin so that the edges of the pastry overlap the top of the tin. Place the chicken mixture inside the tin on the pastry and fold over the edges of the pastry to enclose the chicken, brushing each layer lavishly with butter. Butter the final sheet of pastry and cut it into strips, then decorate the top of the pie with the strips. Cook in the preheated oven for 20 minutes. At the end of this time, take the pie from the oven, remove the sides of the cake tin, brush the edges of the pie with butter and return to the oven for 25 minutes or until the outside is golden brown. If the top starts to darken too much, cover with foil.

To serve, slide the pie off the base with a metal spatula and onto a warm serving dish.

Preparation time: 15–20 minutes
Cooking time: 45 minutes

Shortcrust Variation

675 g (1½ lb) shortcrust
  pastry
22.8 cm (9 in) diameter,
  deep-sided flan tin
beaten egg for glazing
chicken filling (see above)

Heat the oven to 350°F (180°C, gas mark 4). Take two thirds of the pastry and roll it out so that its diameter is about 7.5–10 cm (3–4 in) bigger than the flan ring, and large enough to cover the sides. Lift the pastry into the ring, leaving a little at the top, and press it into shape to prevent air pockets. Spoon in the chicken filling, fold the edges of the pastry over and brush it with beaten egg. Roll out the remaining pastry to a piece large enough to cover the chicken and seal the edges of the pie. Decorate and brush with beaten egg. Make a hole in the centre of the pie to allow the air to escape, and refrigerate until ready to use. Before cooking, brush the pie with egg glaze again and cook in the preheated oven for 20 minutes. Remove the flan ring, brush the edges of the pie with glaze and cook for 25 minutes at 375°F (190°C, gas mark 5). If the pastry gets too brown, cover the top with foil.

Preparation time: 20 minutes
Cooking time: 45 minutes

CHICKEN IN A PUMPKIN

Illustrated on page 67

Serves 6

1 chicken
1 large pumpkin
salt and black pepper
2 tablespoons chopped
  parsley
1 tablespoon fresh tarragon
50 g (2 oz) butter
120 g (4 oz) long grain rice

Apart from looking good (and saving on washing up!), this method keeps the chicken beautifully moist.

Slice the top off the pumpkin and hollow it out, leaving a thick layer of flesh. Season the inside. Stuff the chicken with the parsley, tarragon and butter. Place the chicken inside the pumpkin and put the top back on. Wrap in foil and bake in the oven for 1 hour. Remove from the oven and add the rice — around the chicken in the pumpkin — and some salt. Bake for another ¾–1 hour until the rice is tender.

Preparation and cooking time: 2 hours

CHICKEN PITTA

Makes 8

450 g (1 lb) cooked chicken
1 egg
1 teaspoon ground
    coriander
1 teaspoon ground cumin
6 tablespoons double cream
30 g (1 oz) flaked almonds,
    toasted
50 g (2 oz) dried apricots,
    chopped
salt and black pepper
8 pitta halves

Only a few years ago pitta bread was a strange novelty you came across in Greek restaurants: now we nearly always have some at home, and it's popular with all age groups. Look out for the mini version too — very useful for buffet eating. It can be kept wrapped in the freezer and put straight into the oven to defrost when needed. This particular filling is delicious in its own right, and if you substituted 300 ml (½ pint) of thin béchamel for the egg and cream it would be a great way of using left-over turkey, served with rice.

Shred the chicken. In a bowl combine the egg, coriander, cumin and double cream and mix well. Add the shredded chicken, toasted almonds and dried apricots, and season with salt and freshly ground black pepper. Put 2 tablespoons in each pitta half, wrap in foil and heat on the barbecue or in the oven for 15 minutes at 350°F (180°C, gas mark 4).

Preparation time: 10 minutes
Cooking time: 15 minutes

BAKED CHICKEN BREASTS WITH TOMATO

Illustrated on page 76

Serves 6

6 chicken breasts
275 g (10 oz) can sliced
    mushrooms
2 cloves garlic, finely
    chopped (optional)
400 g (14 oz) tin chopped
    Italian tomatoes
pinch of oregano and thyme
salt and black pepper
3 tablespoons fresh
    breadcrumbs
50 g (2 oz) Gruyère cheese,
    freshly grated

This basic recipe is a marvellous way of perking up chicken breasts, which can sometimes be rather bland. Add or subtract as you wish: the mushrooms aren't essential and it would be delicious with some asparagus or tarragon for a change. The cheese and breadcrumbs give a nice crunchy topping: Gruyère gives a better taste and texture but Cheddar will do it if it's all you have.

Heat the oven to 350°F (180°C, gas mark 4). Remove the skin from the chicken breasts if necessary, and trim any fat. Place the chicken on the base of a gratin dish, add the drained

mushrooms, and garlic if using. Add a pinch of oregano and thyme to the tomatoes and add these to the dish. Season, and mix well. Combine the breadcrumbs and Gruyère and sprinkle over the chicken and tomato. Cook in the preheated oven for 25 minutes, or until the chicken is tender. Ten minutes before the end of cooking, turn the oven up to 400°F (200°C, gas mark 6) to crisp the breadcrumbs.

Preparation and cooking time: 30 minutes

TANDOORI CHICKEN DRUMSTICKS

Illustrated on page 34

Serves 6

12 chicken drumsticks,
    skinned
1 teaspoon salt
6 tablespoons red wine
    vinegar
2 onions, chopped
2 cloves garlic, finely
    chopped
4 tablespoons mustard
    (with seeds)
2 teaspoons turmeric
2 teaspoons ground cumin
2 teaspoons ground
    cinnamon
½ teaspoon black pepper

Make sure the marinade permeates the meat: if you're in a hurry and don't have time to marinate it overnight leave it at room temperature for 6 hours.

Make several slits in each drumstick with the point of a sharp knife. Place the drumsticks in a large flat ovenproof dish and season with a little salt. Combine the vinegar with all the other ingredients and mix well. Spread this marinade on the chicken drumsticks, cover the dish tightly with foil or with a lid and place it in the refrigerator for at least 24 hours.
Heat the oven to 400°F (200°C, gas mark 6). Place the chicken drumsticks on a rack with a baking tray positioned underneath it to catch the juices and cook for 50–60 minutes, or until the juices run clear when the flesh is pricked with a fork. Cooking the drumsticks in

this way means that the fat will drain away and the tandoori coating will crisp up. Serve immediately, or remove from the oven and leave the chicken to cool.

Preparation time: 5 minutes
Marinating time: 24 hours
Cooking time: 50–60 minutes

CHICKEN PILAU

Illustrated on page 48

Serves 6

6 chicken breasts
30 g (1 oz) butter
2 tablespoons vegetable or
    sesame oil
1 onion, chopped
1 clove garlic, chopped
340 g (12 oz) long grain rice
6 tablespoons Chinese red
    barbecue sauce
600 ml (1 pint) chicken
    stock
85 g (3 oz) raisins
5 slices ham, cut into strips
5 sticks chopped celery,
    blanched
1 bunch spring onions,
    chopped and blanched
120 g (4 oz) French beans,
    chopped and blanched

This is perfect for late nights – filling but not heavy or rich: delicious served with some good chutney. Vary it by using pork, or add strips of thin omelette and a dash of soy sauce for an East Indian flavour.

Skin and chop the chicken breasts, and lightly brown them in the butter and oil. Add the chopped onion and cook until lightly browned (about 10 minutes) and then add the garlic and fry for a further 2 minutes. Add the rice and stir, making sure the grains are well coated in oil. Stir in the barbecue sauce and chicken stock. Bring to a boil and simmer gently for 15 minutes until almost all the liquid has been absorbed. Stir in the remaining ingredients, heat through and serve.

Advance preparation: You can set this dish aside after simmering for 10 minutes, cool and place in the refrigerator. Reheat gently for 5 minutes, stir in the remaining ingredients, heat through and serve.
Preparation time: 20 minutes
Cooking time: 30 minutes

RAISED GAME PIE

Illustrated on page 67

Serves 8

For the pastry
500 g (1 lb) plain flour
½ teaspoon salt
150 ml (¼ pint) water
150 g (5 oz) lard, cut into
    chunks
melted butter for greasing
pink and green food
    colouring (optional)

For the filling
250 g (8 oz) sausagemeat
500 g (1 lb) uncooked
    pheasant *or* partridge,
    and turkey (not more
    than half turkey)
1 garlic clove, crushed
salt and black pepper
1 teaspoon fresh parsley,
    chopped
1 teaspoon fresh thyme,
    chopped
2 hardboiled eggs, chopped
6 rashers of bacon, without
    rind and chopped
    coarsely
300 ml (½ pint) game stock
    (made with the bones) or
    canned consommé
1 egg yolk
1½ teaspoons aspic powder
    or gelatine
sprigs of parsley to garnish

This delicious game pie is perfect for the autumn, or filled with chicken and ham for a summer lunch. You can buy specially designed, fluted, oval tins with removable sides, but they are expensive. A 13 cm (5 in) diameter loose-bottomed cake tin does just as well.

Sift the flour and salt into a bowl. Heat the water and lard in a saucepan over a low heat to melt the fat. Bring the liquid to a boil, pour into the flour and mix quickly to a dough. Add a little hot water if necessary but don't make the pastry sticky. Knead lightly until smooth, cover with a damp cloth and stand in a warm place for 10–15 minutes.

Brush the tin generously with melted butter. Divide the pastry roughly into three. Keep the piece for the lid covered in a warm place. Roll out one piece and use it to line the bottom of the tin. Roll the second piece and line the sides, pressing joins together to seal.

Mix the garlic into the sausagemeat and season. Cut the game and turkey into large chunks. Use half the sausagemeat to make a layer at the bottom of the pie, then make a layer of half the mixed game and turkey. Sprinkle with some of the herbs and season well. Add the eggs and some of the bacon, then add the remaining sausagemeat, game and turkey. Add more herbs and seasoning as

you go. Top with the rest of the bacon, and moisten with 2 tablespoons of stock.

Heat the oven to 350°F (180°C, gas mark 4). Roll out the remaining pastry and cut a generous circle for the top of the pie. Seal the lid by dampening the edges of the pastry and nipping them together decoratively. Make a hole in the centre of the pie about 1 cm (½ in) wide, and brush the pastry with egg yolk.

From the spare pastry cut out leaf shapes and mark them with a leaf pattern using the back of a knife. Form the acorns and use a bottle top to cut out acorn cups. Wrap the cups round the acorns and stick them onto the pie. Paint the acorns and leaves with food colouring if you wish. Bake in the preheated oven for 1½–1¾ hours. (You may have to cover it with foil if it gets too brown). Remove from the oven and allow to cool.

Mix the aspic powder or gelatine with the remaining stock, following the manufacturer's instructions. Pour this mixture through the hole in the top of the pie (an icing bag is useful here). Chill for about an hour and add more jelly. Chill again. Remove the tin at the last minute and garnish the pie with parsley.

Preparation time: 45 minutes
Cooking time: 1½–1¾ hours

STIR-FRIED CHICKEN AND MANGO

Illustrated on page 78

Serves 4

Serves 4

450 g (1 lb) chicken breast
3 fresh mangoes or
1 × 425 g (15 oz) tin
mango
225 g (8 oz) tin bamboo
shoots
3 tablespoons vegetable oil
4 tablespoons yellow bean
sauce
120 g (4 oz) bean sprouts

This has an Eastern flavour without being too spicy. The ideal way to stir-fry is to use a wok over a gas flame: the food cooks more evenly and doesn't sit in the oil. You can add any kind of vegetable – green beans, mange-tout and so on – but as stir-frying is so quick you need the best and freshest ingredients. Fresh mango rather than tinned, for instance, makes all the difference. Serve with rice.

Skin and trim the chicken breast and cut it into thin strips about 5 cm (2 in) long. Peel and stone the mangoes (or drain tinned mango) and cut the fruit up into strips. Drain the bamboo shoots. Put all of the ingredients on a tray until ready to serve.

Heat the vegetable oil in the wok and,

when it is very hot, add the chicken. Stir fry until just tender (be careful not to overcook the chicken as it will become dry and stringy). Add the mango, bamboo shoots and yellow bean sauce and cook for a further 2 minutes, stirring with a wooden spoon. Add the bean sprouts and cook until they are warm but still crisp. Transfer to a warmed serving dish and serve at once.

Advance preparation: Stir-fry food does not improve if kept warm in the oven, so you will have to cook and serve straight from the wok. If you have more than one wok you could have several dishes cooking at the same time.
Preparation time: 8 minutes
Cooking time: 10 minutes

CHICKEN AND ORANGE PARCELS

Illustrated on page 29

Serves 6

6 chicken breasts, trimmed
6 slices of orange, halved,
with the peel on
pinch saffron threads
50 g (2 oz) butter
225 g (½ lb) onions
340 g (12 oz) long grain rice
900 ml (1½ pint) chicken
stock
salt and black pepper
50 g (2 oz) pine nuts
450 g (1 lb) leeks

Silver foil really comes into its own in this recipe: ideal if you're catering for large numbers, as the main course is in one container and you don't need to worry about it getting cold as you serve everyone. The foil makes the parcels perfect for a silver wedding or, with a gold ribbon tied round and the saffron rice inside, they would be terrific for a golden one too. Try to find saffron threads because powdered saffron is not as strongly flavoured and it is sometimes diluted with other powders. It is expensive, of course – turmeric would be a cheaper alternative.

Soak the saffron in an egg cup of hot water for half an hour. Peel and chop the onions and cook them in 30 g (1 oz) of butter over a low heat, until soft. Add the rice, stirring very gently until every grain is coated with butter, and sauté, still stirring, until transparent. Pour in the stock, add seasoning and stir well. Cover the pan tightly, turn the heat to very low and let the rice cook for 10 minutes. While the rice is cooking, fry the pine nuts in 15 g (½ oz) butter for a few minutes. Take the rice off the heat and leave for a further 5 minutes with the lid on the pan. Stir the saffron solution, both liquid and threads, and the pine nuts into the cooked rice.

Trim the leeks and cut into julienne strips – about 3.8 cm (1½ in) long. Melt 15 g (½ oz) of

butter over a low heat and cook the leeks, stirring occasionally, until soft but not mushy. Season with salt and pepper. Meanwhile skin and trim the chicken breasts.

Preheat the oven to 350°F (180°C, gas mark 4). Brush six pieces of foil with butter for the chicken, rice and leeks. Place one sixth of the rice in the centre of each piece of foil, then one sixth of the leeks, and top with a chicken breast. Decorate each parcel with two half slices of orange, close the foil and cook the chicken parcels in the preheated oven for 30 minutes. Keep warm until ready to serve and present in the foil wrappers.

Advance preparation: The rice and leeks can be cooked the day before, and the parcels assembled in the morning, but bring them to room temperature before cooking.
Preparation and cooking time: 50 minutes

BEEF, LAMB AND PORK

BŒUF STROGANOFF

675 g (1½ lb) fillet or good
    rump steak
50 g (2 oz) butter
1½ tablespoons vegetable oil
3 onions, finely chopped
340 g (12 oz) button
    mushrooms
salt and black pepper
150 ml (¼ pint) sour cream,
    or double cream with 2
    teaspoons lemon juice

You must use really good quality meat for this classic recipe, and don't overcook it. This is an old but trusted standby when you don't have much time. Serve with rice and a side salad.

Cut the beef into strips approximately 5 cm (2 in) long × 0.6 cm (¼ in) thick. Melt half the butter and oil in a thick-bottomed pan and cook the onion until it is soft and transparent. Add the mushrooms and cook for another minute or two.

Remove the mushroom and onion mixture from the heat and set aside. Melt the remaining fat and cook the meat over a medium heat, moving it around in the pan, until it is evenly cooked. Add the mushrooms and onion, season and mix in the sour cream. Heat through, but do not boil. Serve immediately.

Preparation time: 10 minutes
Cooking time: 15 minutes

GREEK BEEF CASSEROLE

Illustrated on page 16

1.1 kg (2½ lb) good braising
    steak, cut into 2.5 cm
    (1 in) cubes
2 cloves garlic, minced
salt and black pepper
150 ml (¼ pint) red wine
1½ tablespoons olive oil
1 large onion
½ teaspoon ground
    cinnamon
½ teaspoon ground
    coriander
2 × 400 g (14 oz) tins
    chopped tomatoes in
    tomato juice
2 tablespoons tomato purée
150 ml (¼ pint) tomato
    ketchup
bouquet garni
½ teaspoon sugar
2 tablespoons red wine
    vinegar
12 small onions (usually
    sold as pickling onions)
120 g (4 oz) feta cheese

This is a delicious, rich, warming winter dish: a variation on the classic Greek tava. Make sure you brown the meat thoroughly before adding the other ingredients. Served with hot crusty bread and a green salad, it is a substantial main course for an informal dinner.

Put the meat into a bowl with the garlic, salt and pepper. Pour over the wine and marinate for 4 hours, or overnight.
    Heat the oven to 300°F (150°C, gas mark 2). Remove the meat and reserve the marinade for later. In a flameproof casserole, brown the meat in the oil, then add the onion, spices and marinade to it. Cook gently on the hob for 15 minutes, before adding the remaining ingredients (except for the pickling onions and cheese). Bring to a boil, remove from the heat and cook the stew in the preheated oven for 1½ to 2 hours, when the meat should be tender. Peel the small onions and boil for 5 minutes before adding them to the stew. Just

before serving, crumble feta cheese over the top of the stew. Serve when the cheese is just beginning to melt.

Preparation time: 10 minutes
Marinating time: at least 4 hours
Cooking time: 2 hours

STIR-FRIED BEEF AND GINGER

Illustrated on page 78

450 g (1 lb) fillet of beef
225 g (½ lb) mange-tout
30 g (1 oz) root ginger
120 g (4 oz) spring onions
4 tablespoons vegetable oil
soy sauce to taste

Note: *The soy sauce gives a salty flavour, so add to taste.*

Substitute a few drops of sesame oil for a little vegetable oil to give a uniquely oriental flavour.

Trim the beef and cut it into thin strips about 5 cm (2 in) long. String the mange-tout, and peel and finely chop the ginger. Trim and chop the onions.
    Heat the oil in the wok and when it is very hot stir-fry the beef until brown on the outside, but still pink in the middle. Push the

meat to one side of the wok and add the mange-tout. Cook for 2 minutes, add the ginger, spring onions and soy sauce to taste, and cook for another 2 minutes, until the food is hot and crisp. Mix in the beef and stir for a few seconds more. Serve immediately, straight from the wok.

Preparation time: 10 minutes
Cooking time: 5 minutes

BEEF WITH DRIED WILD MUSHROOMS

Illustrated on page 33

Serves 6

1.1 kg (2½ lb) stewing beef, such as chump or blade
20 g (¾ oz) dried wild mushrooms
3 tablespoons corn oil
2 onions, sliced
45 g (1½ oz) butter
45 g (1½ oz) flour
salt and black pepper

Note: *The dried mushrooms to use are French cèpes or Italian porcini.*

It's really worth hunting down the wild dried mushrooms for this recipe: they not only give it the most marvellous taste, but help to produce a beautiful dark mahogany colour. You can use ordinary mushrooms but it's not the same.

Soak the mushrooms in 600 ml (1 pint) of tepid water for 20 minutes. Preheat the oven to 325°F (170°C, gas mark 3).

Trim the beef and dice it. Heat the oil in a frying pan and brown the meat in batches. Remove with a slotted spoon and place in a flameproof casserole. Brown the onions gently in the frying pan — this can take up to 20 minutes — and add them to the meat. Melt the butter, add the flour and stir constantly to form a roux. Drain the mushrooms, and add the mushroom liquid gradually to the roux, stirring constantly. Be careful not to add any sediment that may be at the bottom of the jug. Bring the sauce to a boil, stirring all the time, until it has thickened, then pour the sauce over the meat and season with freshly ground black pepper. Rinse the mushrooms and add them to the casserole. Cook the casserole until just bubbling, cover and cook in the preheated oven for 1¾–2 hours, or until the meat is tender. Remove from the oven and season.

Advance preparation: When reheating, cook the casserole on the hob until just bubbling. Transfer to a preheated oven, covered, for 30 minutes or until it is heated through.
Preparation time: 30 minutes
Cooking time: 1¾–2 hours

Pie Variation

340 g (12 oz) puff pastry
beaten egg for glazing
2 litre (3–3½ pint) pie dish
beef filling (see above), cooked for only 1¼–1½ hours

Roll out the pastry until it is 0.6–1.2 cm (½–¼ in) thick and 5 cm (2 in) larger than the lip of the pie dish. Cut a strip of pastry 2.5 cm (1 in) wide, brush the rim of the dish with beaten egg, line with the pastry strip, and brush this with egg glaze. Put the beef filling into the dish and set a pie funnel in the centre. Place the remaining pastry over the casserole, seal it, knock up the edges, and make a hole in the centre to allow steam to escape. Decorate as desired and refrigerate until ready to cook. Cook in a preheated oven at 425°F (210°C, gas mark 7) for 20–25 minutes.

Preparation time: 10 minutes
Cooking time: 20–25 minutes

BEEF, POTATO AND OLIVE SALAD

Serves 6

12 slices of rare roast beef
900 g (2 lb) small new potatoes
120 g (¼ lb) pitted green olives
1 sprig of mint
1 clove garlic, crushed
150 ml (¼ pint) olive oil
2 tablespoons cider vinegar
1 × 150 g (5 oz) carton natural yoghurt
1 tablespoon mild wholegrain mustard
salt and black pepper
1 bunch watercress

This excellent salad makes a little beef go a very long way, and it would be perfect for lunch, or to serve as part of a summer buffet. Leave out the olives if you don't like the taste of them. You could try adding some capers or some anchovies instead, both rather sophisticated tastes too.

Scrub the potatoes (or scrape them if you prefer) and put them into a pan of cold salted water to which you have added the mint. Bring slowly to the boil and cook until just tender — about 10 minutes.

Slice the beef into strips, and slice most of the olives, leaving a few aside. In a bowl, combine all the other ingredients except the watercress and, when the potatoes are lukewarm, coat the potatoes, beef and olives with the dressing. Pile the salad onto a bed of watercress and garnish with the remaining olives.

Preparation time: 30 minutes

LAMB STUFFED WITH FENNEL

Serves 6–8

4 tablespoons olive oil
2 onions, finely chopped
900 g (2 lb) fennel bulbs, trimmed and sliced
300 ml (½ pint) vegetable stock
2 kg (4½ lb) boned shoulder of lamb
1 teaspoon dried oregano
8 cloves garlic, finely chopped
120 g (¼ lb) thinly sliced Parma ham
3 baby carrots, diced
1 onion, sliced
300 ml (½ pint) dry Italian wine
salt and black pepper
2 bay leaves
2 tomatoes, preferably plum-type, chopped and seeds removed
parsley to garnish

Here a stuffed shoulder of lamb is braised in white wine, with fennel, carrots, garlic, onion and herbs. The tender meat is also delicious cold.

Heat the oven to 350°F (180°C, gas mark 4). Heat half of the oil in a frying pan, add the chopped onion and cook for 10 minutes. Add the fennel and mix with the onion. Cook for 2 minutes longer, then add half of the stock. Cover and cook for 30 minutes. Remove the lid and allow to cool.

Sprinkle the lamb with the oregano and half of the garlic. Cover the lamb with the Parma ham and spread it with half the fennel mixture. Sprinkle with the remaining garlic. Roll up the lamb and tie with string.

Heat the remaining oil in a flameproof casserole, add the lamb and brown on all sides, basting the meat with the oil – this takes about 10 minutes. Add the carrots and sliced onion and brown for 2–3 minutes. Add the wine, bay leaves, tomatoes and the remaining fennel mixture to the casserole and season with salt and black pepper. Place the casserole in the oven and cook for 30 minutes. Reduce the oven to 325°F (170°C, gas mark 3) and cook, covered, for 1 hour.

Remove the lamb from the casserole and leave to rest in a warm place for 10–20 minutes. Meanwhile, take out the bay leaves and purée the sauce in the blender until smooth, adding the rest of the stock to thin it if necessary. Slice some of the meat and present on a dish with the sauce and the rest of the meat, garnished with parsley.

Preparation time: 40 minutes
Cooking time: 2½ hours

LAMB CHOPS STUFFED WITH PEACHES

Serves 6

6 double lamb loin chops, chined
1–2 onions, chopped
12 dried peaches, chopped
3 tablespoons finely chopped parsley
4 teaspoons olive oil
2 teaspoons dried mixed herbs
2 cloves garlic, finely chopped
2 teaspoons grated lemon rind
2 teaspoons lemon juice
6 sprigs fresh mint to garnish

This impressive dish is ideal for entertaining because the chops can be prepared in advance and then left to cook while you serve the first course.

Scrape the meat from the ends of the two bones on each chop. Cut a pocket horizontally to the bone in each chop. Put the onions and dried peaches in a food processor and process until finely chopped. Use this mixture to stuff the chops.

Mix together the parsley, olive oil, mixed herbs, garlic and lemon rind and juice. Press evenly over both sides of each chop. Cover and chill for at least 1 hour.

Heat the oven to 425°F (220°C, gas mark 7). Arrange the chops in a baking tray and cook in the preheated oven for 25 minutes or until tender (the juice should run pink when the flesh is pierced). Leave to stand for 5–10 minutes. To serve, cut the chops in half between the bones. If you like, put cutlet frills on the ends of the bones.

Advance preparation: The chops can be stuffed and coated the day before. Bring them to room temperature before cooking.
Preparation time: 45 minutes
Chilling time: At least 1 hour
Cooking time: 25 minutes

ITALIAN SAUSAGES WITH CABBAGE

Serves 6

6 fresh Italian sausages
2 tablespoons vegetable oil
900 g (2 lb) firm green cabbage, shredded
300 ml (½ pint) dry white wine
2 teaspoons dried oregano
1 teaspoon dried basil
1 × 400 g (14 oz) tin flageolet beans, drained
salt and black pepper

Italian sausages, with their sweet-spicy flavourings, go very well with cabbage. Here the sausages are braised with green cabbage in white wine, and tender beans are added.

In a large frying pan, brown the sausages, turning them so that they colour evenly. Set aside. Heat the oil in a large flameproof casserole, add the cabbage and fry for 2–3 minutes. Stir in the white wine and herbs, then add the sausages, burying them in the cabbage. Cover and cook over a low heat for 30 minutes or until the cabbage is tender.

Add the flageolet beans and seasoning. Heat through gently, and serve hot.

Preparation time: 10 minutes
Cooking time: 1 hour

LAMB PITTA

Illustrated on page 64

Makes 8

450 g (1 lb) minced raw
    lamb
2 medium-sized onions
3 tablespoons oil
2 teaspoons tomato purée
2 tablespoons dried mint
2 teaspoons Worcester
    sauce
150 ml (¼ pint) chicken
    stock
salt and black pepper
4 pitta breads, halved

*A delicious filling for the wonderful pitta bread —
so much more exciting than a sandwich but
equally convenient! You could also make this with
left-over cooked lamb, as a change from the usual
shepherd's pie.*

Peel and chop the onions. Heat the oil and add
the onions. Cook, stirring occasionally, until
they have softened, then add the minced lamb
and cook until it is brown all over. Add the
tomato purée, dried mint, Worcester sauce and
chicken stock. Season with salt and freshly
ground black pepper. Cook over a gentle heat
for 20 minutes, stirring occasionally, until the
lamb is tender.

Put 2 tablespoons of the filling into each
pitta half, wrap in foil and heat on the
barbecue or in the oven.

Advance preparation: The lamb can be
cooked in advance and reheated in the oven
for 15 minutes at 350°F (180°C, gas mark 4).
Preparation time: 5 minutes
Cooking time: 30 minutes

LAMB KORMA

Illustrated on page 40

Serves 6

900 g (2 lb) trimmed
    shoulder of lamb
5 tablespoons oil
225 g (½ lb) onions
2.5 cm (1 in) ginger
1 clove garlic, crushed
2 teaspoons ground
    coriander
2 teaspoons ground cumin
2 teaspoons turmeric
½ teaspoon cinnamon
¼ teaspoon cayenne pepper
1 teaspoon salt
150 ml (¼ pint) single cream
6 tablespoons water
1 × 225 g (½ lb) tart cooking
    apple, grated

*Although this has a distinctly Indian taste and is
pleasantly spicy, it is not too hot, and even feeble
palates like mine will enjoy it. As well as rice, it
would be fun to serve it with the traditional
accompaniments: chutney, sliced mild onion,
chopped tomato, raita (yoghurt and cucumber) and
papadums.*

Heat the oven to 325°F (170°C, gas mark 3).
Heat the oil in a flameproof casserole and
brown the meat. Remove with a slotted spoon
and set aside. Finely chop the onion, add it to
the pan and cook for 10 minutes. Stir in the
ground spices and seasoning. Pour in the
cream and 6 tablespoons water, mix well, then
add the browned meat and the grated apple.
Bring the sauce to a boil, cover and transfer to
the oven for 1½–2 hours.

Advance preparation: The curry can be
cooked the day before and refrigerated
overnight. The easiest way to reheat it is to
bring the sauce to boiling point (but don't
allow it to continue to boil as the meat will
toughen), then transfer it to a preheated oven
325°F (170°C, gas mark 3) for half an hour.
Preparation time: 20 minutes
Cooking time: 1½–2 hours

SWEET AND SOUR BAKED PORK

Illustrated on page 76

Serves 6

3 × 225 kg (½ lb) pork fillets
2 small onions
2 tablespoons oil
2 tablespoons brown sugar
2 tablespoons French
    mustard
2 tablespoons tomato purée
4 tablespoons stock
2 tablespoons Worcester
    sauce
4 tablespoons lemon juice
2 tablespoons red wine
    vinegar
2 tablespoons soy sauce
salt and black pepper

*Serve this with baked or mashed potatoes. The
quick-and-easy sweet and sour mixture would be
equally good over pork chops or cubed shoulder
pork, but would need longer cooking — up to 1
hour. You could also use it with shellfish.*

Heat the oven to 350°F (180°C, gas mark 4).
Chop the onions very finely. Heat the oil, add
the onions and cook for a few minutes.
Combine all the remaining ingredients (except
the pork) in a bowl, and add to the onions.
Allow this mixture to come to a boil and
simmer for 2–3 minutes while you trim any
fat from the pork. Place the meat in an
ovenproof dish and spoon over the sauce.
Cover, and bake in the oven for 25 minutes or
until the pork is tender.

To serve, slice the pork thickly and lay the
slices, overlapping, in the centre of a dish.
Spoon the sauce around the meat and place
any vegetables you are serving with the dish
on either side. Serve at once.

Preparation time: 5–10 minutes
Cooking time: 25 minutes

PISTACHIO PORK IN FILO PASTRY

Serves 6

85 g (3 oz) butter
120 g (4 oz) mushrooms, finely chopped
2 tablespoons finely chopped parsley
40 g (1½ oz) shelled pistachio nuts, chopped
675 g (1½ lb) minced pork
1 tablespoon brandy
salt and black pepper
12 sheets filo pastry

Filo pastry makes an ideal crisp wrapping for a filling of pork, pistachio nuts and mushrooms, subtly flavoured with brandy. Serve the parcel whole, and cut it into slices at the table.

Heat the oven to 400°F (200°C, gas mark 6). Melt 30 g (1 oz) of the butter in a frying pan and cook the mushrooms until the moisture from them has completely evaporated. Allow to cool, then stir in the parsley. Mix together the pistachio nuts, minced pork, brandy and seasoning.

Layer seven sheets of filo pastry, brushing each layer with melted butter. Place one-third of the mushrooms along one end of the pastry, cover with the meat mixture in a sausage shape and top with the rest of the mushrooms. Roll up the pastry around the meat, brushing with butter as you go.

Layer four sheets of filo pastry on a greased baking tray, brushing each layer with melted butter. Place the pork roll, seam side down, on top and wrap the filo pastry around it. Turn the parcel over and make two holes on top to allow the steam to escape. Brush with butter. Cut the remaining sheet of filo into ribbons and place them on top of the pork roll. Dot with melted butter. Bake in the preheated oven for 25 minutes or until a skewer inserted into the centre comes out hot. Serve hot.

Preparation time: 1 hour plus cooling
Cooking time: 25 minutes

MÉDAILLONS OF PORK IN MUSTARD SAUCE

Serves 6

3 pork fillets, each weighing 225 g (½ lb)
30 g (1 oz) butter
1 tablespoon vegetable oil
4 shallots, very finely chopped
300 ml (½ pint) dry white wine
300 ml (½ pint) chicken stock
150 ml (¼ pint) double cream
1 tablespoon Dijon mustard
1 tablespoon coarse-grain mustard
1 tablespoon raspberry vinegar
salt and black pepper

Tender pieces of pork fillet are sautéed and then served in a creamy wine-based sauce that contains two mustards – Dijon and coarse-grain, and fruity raspberry vinegar.

Cut each pork fillet across into four pieces. Place them, one at a time, between two sheets of clingfilm and pound to flatten. Heat the butter in a large frying pan. Sauté the slices of pork for 4 minutes on each side, in batches if necessary, then remove from the pan and keep warm. Add the shallots to the pan and cook for 1 minute or until softened. Stir in the wine and chicken stock and reduce to half the original quantity. Add the cream, stirring. Reduce until the sauce has thickened.

Reduce the heat and stir in the two mustards and the vinegar. Do not boil after adding the mustard as this would make the sauce granular. Season. Return the pork to the pan and heat through gently, then serve with steamed vegetables.

Preparation time: 20 minutes
Cooking time: 25 minutes

CHINESE GINGER PORK

Serves 6

900 g (2 lb) chard or Chinese leaf
2 tablespoons vegetable oil
3–4 tablespoons ginger and orange sauce
450 g (1 lb) smoked loin of pork, cut into thin strips
50 g (2 oz) tinned water chestnuts, cut in half
2 tablespoons flaked almonds, toasted

This savoury dish of pork and green vegetable has a very appealing combination of flavours, colours and textures. Serve it very hot, as part of an oriental feast, and maybe eat with chopsticks?

Wash the chard or Chinese leaf. Cut the white stalks from the green leaves and slice the stalks; shred the leaves. Heat the oil in a frying pan or wok, add the stalks and stir-fry for 1 minute. Add 2 tablespoons ginger and orange sauce and cook for 2 minutes, then add the pork and water chestnuts. Continue to cook for 5–8 minutes, adding the remaining ginger and orange sauce as necessary.

Meanwhile, in a saucepan, bring about 5 cm (2 in) of water to a boil, add the shredded chard or Chinese leaves and cook until tender but still firm. When the pork is cooked, add the toasted almonds. Transfer the pork mixture to a serving dish and place the chard or Chinese leaves around it. Serve immediately.

Preparation time: 20 minutes
Cooking time: 9–12 minutes

GLAZED HAM

Illustrated on page 73

Serves 12–16

1 × 3.6 kg (8 lb) cooked
  ham or gammon
cloves
50 g (2 oz) French mustard
450 g (1 lb) soft brown
  sugar
225 ml (8 fl oz) sherry (or
  Madeira)
75 ml (3 fl oz) water

Note: *As an alternative to
mustard, brush the surfaces
of the ham with honey and
sugar glaze. Bake at 450°F
(230°C, gas mark 8) for 30
minutes.*

*A glazed ham sitting on the sideboard looks as
good as it tastes – hot or cold – and makes an
excellent alternative at Christmas or in a buffet.
For dramatic effect it can be flambéed.*

Heat the oven to 400°F (200°C, gas mark 6).
Remove the skin from the ham, leaving about
0.6 cm (¼ in) layer of fat. Score the fat in a criss-
cross diamond pattern, and stick a clove into
the point of each diamond. Place the ham in a
shallow roasting pan and spread the mustard
over the top and sides of the ham.
    Meanwhile put the sugar, sherry and water
into a saucepan and bring to a boil. Remove

the syrup from the heat and pour around the
ham. Bake the ham in the oven for 1 hour,
basting frequently with the glaze.

Preparation time: 10 minutes
Cooking time: 1 hour

PORK AND APRICOT CASSEROLE

Illustrated on page 17

Serves 6

1.1 kg (2½ lb) lean shoulder
  of pork, chopped
150 g (5 oz) plump dried
  apricots
600 ml (1 pint) water
2 tablespoons corn oil
45 g (1½ oz) butter
45 g (1½ oz) flour
1 chicken stock cube
salt and black pepper

Note: *If you are buying the
meat from a butcher, get it in
one piece rather than cut
into cubes, so that you can
trim off the fat yourself.*

*The pork must be really well cooked so that it
melts in the mouth. Apricots keep the casserole
light, but you could ring the changes with prunes
and a dash of soy sauce.*

Place the dried apricots in a saucepan with
600 ml (1 pint) water, bring to a boil and
simmer gently for 30 minutes or until tender.
    Heat the oven to 325°F (170°C, gas mark
3). Heat the oil in a frying pan and brown the
pork in batches. Remove the meat with a
slotted spoon and place in an ovenproof
casserole.
    Drain the apricots and set them aside. In a
pan, melt the butter and add the flour to it,
stirring constantly to form a roux. If necessary
add water to the apricot juice so that you have
600 ml (1 pint) of liquid. Gradually add the
liquid to the roux, whisking all the time. Bring

the sauce to a boil, stirring constantly and boil
until the sauce has thickened. Crumble the
stock cube into the sauce, whisking well. Pour
the sauce over the meat in the dish, season
with salt and pepper and cook until just
bubbling. Cover and cook in the preheated
oven for 1–1½ hours, or until the meat is
tender. Add the apricots 30 minutes before the
end of cooking time.

Advance preparation: Reheat the cooked
casserole in a saucepan. Add the apricots to
the pan, season to taste, bring to a boil and
transfer to an ovenproof dish. Place in the
preheated oven at 325°F (170°C, gas mark 3)
for 30 minutes or until the casserole is heated
through.
Preparation time: 45 minutes
Cooking time: 1–1½ hours

CANNELLINI AND BACON CASSEROLE

Serves 6

2 × 400 g (14 oz) tin
  cannellini beans
10 rashers streaky bacon
2 onions, finely chopped
2 cloves garlic (optional)
1 × 400 g (14 oz) tin
  tomatoes
1 × 400 g (14 oz) can sliced
  mushrooms, drained
1 × 400 g (14 oz) tin celery
  hearts, drained
salt and black pepper

*An absolutely delicious speedy meal, using
ingredients from your store cupboard, including the
much underrated cannellini beans. Add any kind
of tinned vegetables you have in the store
cupboard, and don't forget it's much easier to cut
bacon with kitchen scissors.*

Remove the rind from the bacon and cut into
strips across. Cook in a flameproof casserole
until the bacon begins to crisp, then add the

chopped onions and garlic and cook for
another 3–4 minutes. Add the cannellini
beans, tomatoes, sliced mushrooms and celery
hearts and season. Mix well and simmer for 5
minutes. Serve immediately.

Preparation time: 5 minutes
Cooking time: 15 minutes

MAIN VEGETARIAN DISHES

VEGETABLE TERRINE

Serves 6

225 g (8 oz) frozen spinach, defrosted
425 g (15 oz) can cannellini beans, drained
2 tablespoons oil
1 onion, chopped
2 cloves garlic (optional)
175 g (6 oz) ricotta or blended cottage cheese
3 eggs, beaten
salt and black pepper
lemon juice
120 g (4 oz) crème fraîche

Note: *The terrine should be easy to slice; use a carving knife or a fish filleting knife.*

This is delicious served hot with piquant Tomato sauce (page 139) and a salad as a light lunch no-meat main course, or in smaller portions as a cold starter for 8 people.

Heat the oven to 400°F (200°C, gas mark 6). Line a 1 litre (1¾ pint) pâté tin (preferably one that has collapsible sides) with greaseproof paper and brush the base and sides with oil. Chop the onion and cook in oil until transparent. Add crushed garlic, if using, for the last 5 minutes. Blend or process the beans with the onion, and add 50 g (2 oz) ricotta or blended cottage cheese and one egg. Blend well and season. Set aside.

Blend the defrosted spinach with the crème fraîche and the rest of the ricotta, and add a squeeze of lemon juice, 2 beaten eggs and seasoning.

Pour the cannellini mixture into the tin and add the spinach mixture on top. Cook, covered with foil, in a bain-marie for 1 hour, or until a skewer comes out clean from the centre of the terrine. Serve hot, or allow to cool and refrigerate overnight. To serve, turn out onto a board, remove the greaseproof paper and cut into thin slices.

Preparation and cooking time: 1–1¼ hours
Chilling time: 8 hours or overnight

VEGETABLE CRUMBLE

Illustrated on page 17

Serves 4–6

450 g (1 lb) carrots
340 g (¾ lb) mange-tout
225 g (½ lb) green beans
2 Spanish tomatoes, sliced
salt and black pepper
50 g (2 oz) Cheddar cheese, grated
30 g (1 oz) breadcrumbs
30 g (1 oz) flour
30 g (1 oz) butter

This has the most wonderful texture and also looks very pretty in a glass dish. It makes an excellent, filling vegetarian main course, served with Tomato sauce (page 139), if you wish.

Preheat the oven to 350°F (180°C, gas mark 4). Peel and slice the carrots, string the mange-tout, and top and tail the green beans. Blanch the vegetables separately. Layer the vegetables, with the tomatoes, in a transparent soufflé dish – carrots first, then mange-tout, tomatoes and finally green beans. Season each layer with salt and pepper. Rub together the remaining ingredients until they form a crumbly mixture and sprinkle this over the vegetables.

Cook the vegetable crumble in the preheated oven for 30 minutes until the top is golden brown and serve.

Preparation time: 20 minutes
Cooking time: 30 minutes

CANNELLINI CASSEROLE

Serves 4–6

2 × 400 g (14 oz) tin cannellini beans
725 g (1 lb 10 oz) flageolets
50 g (2 oz) butter
50 g (2 oz) flour
600 ml (1 pint) milk
150 ml (¼ pint) double cream
2 cloves garlic, finely sliced
salt and white pepper
fresh parsley

An easy centrepiece for a no-meat meal, served with salad or vegetables, this is also perfect in smaller portions with game or roast meat as an alternative to potatoes.

Melt the butter in a flameproof casserole, add the flour and whisk to form a roux. Gradually add the milk and cream, whisking all the time until the sauce begins to thicken. Then add the sliced garlic. Simmer gently for 15–20 minutes, stirring frequently to make sure the sauce doesn't stick to the bottom of the casserole. Add seasoning and, over a gentle heat, stir in the cannellini beans and flageolets and heat through. Coarsely chop the parsley and fold a little into the beans. Sprinkle the rest over the top just before serving.

Advance preparation: If you make the casserole in advance, don't add the parsley until serving. Reheat the casserole over a gentle heat, or in the oven, at 325°F (170°C, gas mark 3), for 30 minutes, covered.
Cooking time: 30 minutes

VEGETARIAN CHILLI

Serves 6

1 × 675 g (1½ lb) cauliflower
2 tablespoons vegetable oil
1 large onion, chopped
1 tablespoon mild chilli powder
1 teaspoon ground cumin
1 teaspoon ground coriander
salt and black pepper
1 × 400 g (14 oz) tin red kidney
    beans
1 × 400 g (14 oz) tin cannellini
    beans
1–2 tablespoons chopped
    parsley to garnish

Serve this wholesome mixed bean and cauliflower chilli with rice, pasta or potatoes for a well-balanced main dish. A spoonful of Greek-style yoghurt on each serving would be a cooling garnish.

Remove the stalks from the cauliflower and cut it into florets. Cook in boiling water for 10–15 minutes or until tender but not mushy.

Meanwhile, heat the oil in a saucepan, add the onion, spices and seasoning and cook for 5–10 minutes. Drain the red kidney beans and add them to the onions. Leave to cook over a low heat, stirring occasionally. Heat the cannellini beans in a separate pan.

Drain the cauliflower. Reserve one or two florets for garnish and mix the remaining cauliflower and half the drained cannellini beans with the kidney beans. Transfer to a serving dish, garnish the corners with the reserved cauliflower and sprinkle the remaining cannellini beans and the chopped parsley over the top.

Preparation time: 10 minutes
Cooking time: 15 minutes

CHEESE AND VEGETABLE BAKE

Serves 6

340 g (¾ lb) butternut, acorn or
    golden squash
340 g (¾ lb) courgettes
salt and black pepper
15 g (½ oz) butter
½ onion, finely chopped
4 eggs, beaten
120 g (4 oz) Cheddar cheese,
    grated
200 g (7 oz) cream cheese
50 g (2 oz) fine fresh
    breadcrumbs
2 tablespoons finely chopped
    parsley

Rich and satisfying, this savoury bake combines Cheddar and cream cheeses with squash and courgettes. If squash is not available you could use a double quantity of courgettes.

Heat the oven to 350°F (180°C, gas mark 4). Grate the squash and courgettes with their skins. Sprinkle with 2 teaspoons salt and leave to drain for 20 minutes.

Meanwhile, melt the butter in a small pan and cook the onion for 5 minutes, stirring occasionally. In a food processor, blend the eggs, Cheddar cheese, cream cheese, breadcrumbs, parsley and seasoning.

Rinse the salt from the squash and courgettes. Squeeze well and dry on paper towels to remove any excess liquid – this is very important, otherwise you will have a watery dish. Mix the squash, courgettes and onion with the cream cheese mixture and turn into a buttered 1.5 litre (2½ pint) soufflé dish. Bake in the preheated oven for 45 minutes, and serve immediately.

Preparation time: 45 minutes
Cooking time: 45 minutes–1 hour

RICE RING WITH MUSHROOMS

Serves 6

600 ml (1 pint) chicken stock
225 g (½ lb) long grain brown
    rice
4 tablespoons olive oil
6 tablespoons finely grated
    Parmesan cheese
2 red peppers, sliced
2 green peppers, sliced
225 g (½ lb) mushrooms,
    sliced
4 cloves garlic, chopped
1 teaspoon dried oregano
2 tablespoons finely chopped
    parsley
salt and black pepper
1 onion, finely chopped
1 × 225 g (8 oz) tin Italian
    tomatoes, coarsely chopped
1 bay leaf

Here a ring of Parmesan rice is filled with a colourful vegetable mixture and served with a tomato sauce.

Bring the stock to a boil in a saucepan, add the rice and cook, covered, for 30 minutes. By this time, the liquid should have been absorbed, so don't let the rice burn.

Heat the oven to 350°F (180°C, gas mark 4). Mix 2 tablespoons olive oil and the Parmesan cheese into the rice, stirring well. Spoon into a lightly oiled 900 ml (1½ pint) ring mould and press it down firmly. Cover the mould closely with foil and bake in the preheated oven for 10–15 minutes.

Meanwhile, heat 1 tablespoon olive oil in a frying pan and cook the red and green peppers, mushrooms, garlic and herbs for 5 minutes. Add pepper to taste. Remove from the heat and keep hot. In a saucepan, heat the remaining oil and cook the onion until softened. Add the tomatoes and bay leaf and cook for 5 minutes. Season with salt and pepper. Remove the bay leaf and blend the tomato sauce until smooth.

To serve, turn out the rice ring onto a large serving platter, place the pepper mixture in the centre and pour the tomato sauce around.

Preparation time: 20 minutes
Cooking time: 45 minutes

AUBERGINE LASAGNE

Serves 6

900 g – 1.4 kg (2 – 3 lb) aubergines
salt and black pepper
6 large red peppers
3 – 4 tablespoons olive oil
2 onions, diced
4 cloves garlic, finely chopped
1 teaspoon dried oregano
6 tablespoons finely chopped parsley
225 g (½ lb) ricotta cheese
2 tablespoons finely grated Parmesan cheese
1 × 190 g (6½ oz) jar pesto sauce

Although this dish takes a little time to prepare, it is well worth it because it is so good. Everyone will want seconds – and the recipe so they can make the lasagne themselves.

Slice the aubergines, sprinkle them with salt and leave to drain for at least 30 minutes. Heat the grill. Grill and skin the red peppers as described on page 85. Rinse the aubergine slices and dry with paper towels. Place them in the grill pan, brush them with some of the oil and cook them under the preheated grill until they are lightly browned on each side. Set aside. Discard the cores and seeds of the peppers and purée the flesh in a blender or food processor.

Heat the oven to 350°F (180°C, gas mark 4). Heat the remaining oil in a frying pan, add the onions and garlic and cook for 5 minutes or until the onions are tender. Season with black pepper, add the oregano and the red pepper purée and cook for a further 2 minutes. Add the parsley and mix thoroughly.

Mix the ricotta and Parmesan cheeses in a bowl. Brush an oblong baking dish with oil. Place aubergine slices in the bottom, spread with red pepper purée and then the cheese mixture and top with pesto sauce. Repeat the layers twice more. Bake for 30 minutes. Serve hot or cold.

Advance preparation: The lasagne can be assembled the day before and refrigerated. Bring it to room temperature before baking.
Preparation time: 2 hours
Cooking time: 40 minutes

BULGAR AND WILD RICE WITH TOFU

Serves 6 – 8

85 g (3 oz) butter
3 large onions, chopped
225 g (½ lb) wild rice
1.5 litres (2½ pints) chicken stock
225 g (½ lb) bulgar (cracked wheat)
2 tablespoons vegetable oil
½ green pepper, diced
1 carrot, diced
1 stick celery, diced
450 g (1 lb) soft tofu (soya bean curd)
1 teaspoon curry powder
1 teaspoon ground cumin
3 bunches spring onions
1 – 2 tablespoons peeled and grated fresh root ginger
340 g (¾ lb) radishes, sliced
salt and black pepper

This recipe may appear complicated, but it is quite straightforward to make, and much of it can be prepared in advance. It's well worth trying because the textures of the pilaff contrast beautifully with the vegetable and tofu curry and with the gingered radish and onion mixture to make an unusual and colourful dish.

Melt 30 g (1 oz) of the butter in a large saucepan and cook one of the onions until softened. Add the wild rice and stir until it is coated with butter. Add 900 ml (1½ pints) chicken stock and simmer, covered, for 40 minutes, or until the rice is tender and the stock is absorbed.

While the rice is cooking, soften a second onion in 30 g (1 oz) butter in another saucepan. Add the bulgar and stir to coat it with the butter. Add the remaining chicken stock and simmer, covered, for 10 minutes, or until the liquid is absorbed. Remove from the heat and let the bulgar stand, covered, for 10 minutes.

Heat the oil in a frying pan and cook the third onion with the green pepper, carrot and celery for 3 – 5 minutes or until softened. Add the diced tofu and spices and cook, covered, for 5 minutes, stirring occasionally.

Slice the white part of the spring onions and finely chop the green part. Melt the remaining butter in another frying pan over a moderate heat and sauté the white part of the onion, stirring, for 2 minutes. Add the ginger and sauté the mixture for 1 minute. Add the radishes and the green part of the spring onions and sauté the mixture for 3 – 4 minutes.

In a large bowl, combine the wild rice and bulgar, tossing well. Season. Pile the pilaff in the middle of a long serving dish. Place the radish mixture on one side and the tofu mixture on the other side of the pilaff. Serve immediately.

Advance preparation: The pilaff can be made the day before and kept, covered, in the refrigerator. To reheat, place it in a shallow buttered baking dish, cover with foil and bake in a preheated 350°F (180°C, gas mark 4) oven for 15 – 20 minutes. During this time, prepare the radish and tofu mixtures.
Preparation time: 20 minutes
Cooking time: 1 hour

VEGETABLES

CRISPY POTATO SKINS

Illustrated on page 33

several large potatoes,
  baked in the oven
butter
sour cream, to serve

Make plenty: these are always very popular. Cut into small pieces, they are excellent for a buffet.

Heat the oven to 400°F (200°C, gas mark 6) or heat the grill to high. Remove the flesh from the potatoes, leaving a thin layer of skin, and reserve for making another potato dish, such as Rice and Potato Nut Balls (below).
  Spread the potato skins with butter, put them on a baking sheet and cook in the oven for 20 minutes, or under the grill for 5–10 minutes, turning regularly, until they are crisp. Serve immediately with the sour cream.

Advance preparation: They can be cooked in advance and reheated in the oven.
Preparation and cooking time: 25 minutes (oven) or 15 minutes (grill)

RICE AND POTATO NUT BALLS

Illustrated on page 33

Makes 24

450 g (1 lb) cooked potato
3 teaspoons butter,
  softened
4 tablespoons double cream
2 egg yolks
120 g (4 oz) cooked rice
225 g (½ lb) finely chopped
  walnuts, or toasted
  sesame seeds

A great way of using left-over cooked potato (perhaps from the crispy potato skins above). They can be kept hot without spoiling and made smaller would be perfect finger food with a Tomato sauce (page 139).

Heat the oven to 350°F (180°C, gas mark 4). In a bowl, mash the potato to a purée, add the softened butter, double cream and egg yolks. Mix well and add the cooked rice. Shape the mixture into balls and roll each one in the walnuts or sesame seeds. Cook the balls in the preheated oven for 15 minutes and serve.

Preparation time: 10 minutes
Cooking time: 15 minutes

COURGETTE BOATS

Illustrated on page 84

Serves 6

6 small courgettes
1 tablespoon olive oil
1 onion, chopped
6 level tablespoons fresh
  breadcrumbs
2 egg yolks
2 tablespoons Parmesan
  cheese
salt and black pepper

The hollowing out of the courgettes needs care, but they go well with most main courses. I like to do them with Tomato sauce (page 139). Served cold, they are excellent for a summer buffet.

Heat the oven to 375°F (190°C, gas mark 5). Trim and slice the courgettes in half lengthways. Scoop out the seeds and just enough of the flesh to leave a thick shell. Reserve the flesh, sprinkle the boats with salt and set aside for 20 minutes cut-side down.
Wipe dry with a piece of kitchen towel.
  Heat the oil and cook the onion on a gentle heat until it is soft and transparent. Add the courgette flesh, breadcrumbs, egg yolks and cheese and season to taste. Mix well, then pile the filling into the courgette shells. Bake in the preheated oven for 20 minutes.

Preparation time: 25 minutes
Cooking time: 20 minutes

HERBED GARLIC POTATOES

Serves 6

675 g (1½ lb) potatoes
85 g (3 oz) herb and garlic
  cream cheese
300 ml (½ pint) milk
300 ml (½ pint) double
  cream
salt and black pepper
butter for greasing
1 clove garlic, cut in half
40 g (1–2 oz) freshly grated
  Cheddar cheese

Delicious with roast meat and game, the potatoes can be kept hot for up to an hour without spoiling.

Heat the oven to 325°F (170°C, gas mark 3). Peel and thinly slice the potatoes and soak them in cold water for 5 minutes. Blend the cream cheese, milk and cream and season.
  Drain the potatoes and dry them in a clean tea towel. Grease an ovenproof gratin dish with butter and rub the dish with cut garlic. Put in one layer of potatoes and pour over some of the cheese mixture. Continue in layers, keeping the best potatoes for the last layer, and finish with some cream cheese. Sprinkle over the grated cheese and cover the dish with foil. Cook in the preheated oven for 1 hour. Remove the foil, turn the oven up to 350°F (180°C, gas mark 4) and cook for a further 15 minutes, until golden brown.

Preparation time: 20 minutes
Cooking time: 1¼ hours

PARTY RICE

Serves 6

225 g (½ lb) Basmati or other long grain rice
2 tablespoons vegetable oil
600 ml (1 pint) chicken stock
40 g (1½ oz) almonds, blanched and shredded

Note: *The cooking method for long grain rice is the same as for Basmati, but you don't need to wash it first.*

We now know that rice not only tastes good but is nutritious too, and it makes a wonderful accompaniment to many dishes. This recipe is especially successful, and if you use Basmati rice — with its lovely nutty flavour and very delicate texture — you will produce a triumph.

Basmati rice needs to be washed first, in a large bowl with plenty of cold water. Stir the rice round and then carefully pour the cloudy water away. Repeat two or three times and then drain the rice thoroughly in a sieve. Heat the oil in a heavy saucepan with a tight-fitting lid. Sauté the rice very gently in the oil for a minute, making sure that every grain is coated with oil. Pour in the chicken stock and bring the liquid to a boil. Cover the pan tightly, turn the heat to very low and let the rice cook for 12 minutes. Turn off the heat and leave the rice for a further 10 minutes with the lid on the pan, then turn it out into a heated serving dish. Add the almonds to the rice and stir gently with a fork.

Preparation time: 5 minutes
Cooking time: 25 minutes

LEEK AND TOMATO GRATIN

Illustrated on page 84

Serves 6

900 g (2 lb) leeks
400 g (14 oz) tin chopped tomatoes
3 cloves garlic, finely chopped
salt and black pepper
30 g (1 oz) freshly grated Cheddar

Leek and tomato is a great combination and this dish would be a good centre to a vegetarian meal, or a perfect accompaniment to plain meat. You could also purée it and use it as a pasta sauce.

Heat the oven to 350°F (180°C, gas mark 4). Remove the outer leaves from the leeks, cut the ends lengthways and wash well under cold running water. Slice the leeks into 2.5 cm (1 in) pieces and place in an ovenproof dish. Cover them with the tinned tomato and garlic and season with salt and pepper. Cover the dish with foil and cook the vegetables in the preheated oven for 30 minutes, or until the leeks have just softened, but are still firm (*al dente*). Sprinkle over the grated cheese and cook for a further 10 minutes, uncovered, until the cheese is golden brown.

Preparation time: 5 minutes
Cooking time: 40 minutes

TWO-TONE CABBAGE

Illustrated on page 84

Serves 6

450 g (1 lb) red cabbage
450 g (1 lb) white cabbage
150 ml (¼ pint) red wine vinegar
150 ml (¼ pint) dry white wine
2 teaspoons fennel seeds
120 g (4 oz) redcurrant jelly
salt and black pepper

Note: *The cabbage must be cooked separately or the white cabbage will discolour.*

Cabbage — either red or white — is one of my favourite vegetables, and this way of cooking it gives a result that looks as good as it tastes. The two colours are very pretty mixed together, but you could keep them separate if you like and arrange them in rows around the meat. If the cabbages are served separately, add a little butter or sesame oil to the white cabbage at the last minute.

Heat the oven to 350°F (180°C, gas mark 4). Remove the core from the red cabbage and discard; slice the cabbage finely. Place in a small ovenproof casserole with the red wine vinegar, and place in the oven for 30 minutes. Meanwhile, remove the core from the white cabbage and discard; slice the cabbage finely. Put it into another small ovenproof casserole, with the white wine and fennel seeds, and place in the oven with the red cabbage to cook for about 20 minutes.

When the red cabbage has been in for 30 minutes, remove both dishes from the oven. Add the redcurrant jelly to the red cabbage and toss well. Season with salt and freshly ground black pepper. Toss the white cabbage and season with salt and pepper. Return them both to the oven for another 30 minutes.

To serve, mix the two cabbages together and pour the cooking liquid from the white cabbage over the top.

Preparation time: 5 minutes
Cooking time: 1–1¼ hours

BRAISED SPRING ONIONS

Serves 6

250 g (9 oz) spring onions
10 rashers streaky bacon,
 chopped
150 ml (¼ pint) chicken
 stock
1–2 teaspoons lemon juice
salt and black pepper

This is a very light vegetable dish with a lovely 'sweet' taste. It's good to find another use for spring onions – rather than just using them in salads.

Heat the oven to 350°F (180°C, gas mark 4). In a flameproof casserole, lightly fry the bacon. Meanwhile remove any damaged outer leaves from the spring onions and trim the ends. Place the spring onions over the bacon in the casserole, and add the chicken stock and lemon juice. Season with salt and black pepper. Cover the casserole and cook in the preheated oven for 20 minutes.

Preparation time: 10 minutes
Cooking time: 20 minutes

BRAISED FENNEL

Illustrated on page 84

Serves 6

6 bulbs of fennel
300–450 ml (½–¾ pint) hot
 chicken stock
2 tablespoons Pernod or dry
 vermouth
salt and black pepper
2 tablespoons chopped
 chives

Fennel is an under-used vegetable – often only seen sliced in salads – and its special aniseedy flavour is enhanced in this recipe by the addition of Pernod (but substitute dry vermouth if you haven't any).

Heat the oven to 350°F (180°C, gas mark 4). Remove the outer leaves from the fennel bulbs if they look tough or damaged, and cut the fennel into halves (or quarters, if they are large). Place them in the base of an ovenproof dish, pour over the stock and Pernod and season with salt and black pepper. Cover the dish, and cook in the preheated oven for about 40 minutes. Serve with a sprinkling of chopped chives.

Preparation time: 5 minutes
Cooking time: 40 minutes

BRAISED LEEKS

Serves 6

12 medium-sized leeks
nut of butter
black pepper
3 tablespoons stock (or 2
 tablespoons lemon juice
 and 1 tablespoon water)
cream, or Parmesan cheese,
 to serve

This is a very good way of cooking leeks to serve with roast meat. You can also braise them in lemon juice to serve with lighter casseroles, such as chicken or pork (page 109 and page 119).

Trim and wash the leeks thoroughly. If any dirt remains, cut them in half lengthways and wash again. Put the leeks into a colander and pour boiling water over them to blanch, then arrange in a buttered casserole; add pepper and pour over the stock (or lemon mixture). Cover and cook in the oven for about 1 hour. Baste the leeks two or three times during cooking. To serve, dribble a little cream over the leeks, or sprinkle with Parmesan cheese.

Preparation time: 5 minutes
Cooking time: 1 hour

BAKED CHICORY WITH ORANGE AND JUNIPER BERRIES

Serves 6

6 large heads of chicory
2 oranges
150 ml (¼ pint) hot chicken
 stock
18 juniper berries
salt and black pepper

This is good with beef. Omit the orange and berries, and this basic cooking method also works well for celery.

Heat the oven to 350°F (180°C, gas mark 4). Remove any outer damaged leaves from the chicory, then wipe clean. Remove the hard white core from the base of the chicory with a sharp knife. Place the chicory in the base of an ovenproof dish, and grate the rind of one orange over it. Squeeze the oranges and pour the juice, with the stock and juniper berries, over the top. Season with salt and pepper. Cover the dish with foil and cook in the preheated oven for 1½ hours. Chicory discolours as it cools, so serve straightaway.

Preparation time: 10 minutes
Cooking time: 1½ hours

VEGETABLE PURÉES

These have the great advantage that they can be made in advance and then reheated; they can also be kept warm without spoiling for much longer than steamed or boiled vegetables.

The method is basically the same for all purées: the vegetables are cooked until just tender, then blended until smooth with a little butter, or cream, *and seasoning. The exception is potato purée, which should be mashed and beaten with a wooden spoon, and not processed or blended because potatoes become waxy when blended. Any number of vegetables or mixture of vegetables can be puréed.*

Parsnip and Pear Purée

Illustrated on page 84

Serves 6

900 g (2 lb) parsnips
450 g (1 lb) ripe pears
5 tablespoons sour cream
salt and white pepper

This has an unusual sweet taste and goes well with the drier meats — such as turkey and game.

Cook the parsnips, and add the pears for the last 5 minutes — both parsnips and pears should be soft — then drain the mixture. Blend and add the sour cream and seasoning.

Preparation and cooking time: 25 minutes

Leek and Potato Purée

Illustrated on page 40

Serves 6

6 large leeks, chopped
1.1 kg (2½ lb) potatoes
120 g (¼ lb) butter, melted
2 cloves garlic (optional)
150 ml (¼ pint) single cream
salt and black pepper

Try this versatile and more interesting alternative to ordinary mashed potato.

Cook the leeks and potatoes. Melt the butter in a small pan, and add the crushed garlic, if using. Cook for about 2–3 minutes. Blend the leeks with the butter and garlic until the mixture is smooth. Mash the potatoes by hand with the cream, salt and pepper and add them to the leek purée, mixing well.

Preparation and cooking time: 20 minutes

Chestnut and Potato Purée

Serves 6

675 g (1½ lb) potatoes,
    peeled and chopped
425 g (15 oz) can
    unsweetened chestnut
    purée
30 g (1 oz) butter, melted
1 egg
75 ml (3 fl oz) double cream
2 tablespoons dry sherry
salt and black pepper
fresh parsley, chopped

I love the taste of chestnuts and am always glad to find a new way of using them. This easy-to-make rich, creamy purée would go particularly well with roast turkey or poultry. If you're in a rush, you could even use instant mashed potato.

Cook and mash the potatoes by hand, then add butter and mix in the chestnut purée. Beat the egg with a fork, add the cream, sherry and seasoning and beat again. Add this mixture to the chestnut and potato purée. Mix well with a wooden spoon and set aside.

Heat the oven to 350°F (180°C, gas mark 4). Butter a deep-sided vegetable or soufflé dish, stir the purée and transfer it to the buttered dish. Cook in the preheated oven for 25 minutes. Sprinkle with chopped parsley and serve.

Preparation and cooking time: 45 minutes

Broccoli Purée

Illustrated on page 24

Serves 6

600–675 g (1¼–1½ lb)
    broccoli
30 g (1 oz) butter, melted
2–3 tablespoons double
    cream, or crème fraîche
few drops lemon juice
salt and black pepper

This creamy purée keeps hot for up to an hour and could be made successfully with frozen broccoli.

Cook the broccoli and drain. Add the butter, cream and lemon juice, season with salt and black pepper to taste, and blend well.

Preparation and cooking time: 20 minutes

NEW POTATOES WITH CUCUMBER DRESSING

Illustrated on page 31

Serves 6

900 g (2 lb) new potatoes, well scrubbed
½ large cucumber, peeled and grated
6 sprigs fresh mint
300 ml (½ pint) natural yoghurt
salt and black pepper

Note: *The potatoes can be skinned or not, according to your preference.*

When we're having new potatoes, I cook double quantity so as to have some over to make potato salad: it's always a favourite. This refreshing, summery dressing makes a good change from the usual thick mayonnaise.

Place the potatoes in a saucepan of cold salted water and add two sprigs of mint. Bring the water to a boil and cook for 10–15 minutes until the potatoes are tender. Drain and allow to cool, and place on a serving dish.

Whisk the yoghurt in a bowl with a fork. Finely chop the remaining mint leaves and add them to the yoghurt with the grated cucumber. Season with salt and black pepper, mix well and pour over the potatoes.

Advance preparation: The dish can be made several hours in advance. If the water from the cucumber comes to the surface, just pour it off.
Preparation and cooking time: 30 minutes

BULGAR WHEAT SALAD

Illustrated on page 61

Serves 6

175 g (6 oz) bulgar wheat
150 ml (¼ pint) lemon juice
1 tablespoon vegetable oil
1 red pepper, skinned (if you have time), seeded and diced
seeds of 1 pomegranate
salt and black pepper
1 tablespoon chopped mint leaves

I ate bulgar wheat as part of the salad choice in the BBC canteen for years without really knowing what it was, and since discovering its identity I have used it frequently at home. It is a form of nutty-tasting, cracked, pre-cooked wheat – you can mix anything into it, just as you would with rice.

Put the bulgar wheat into a pan, add the lemon juice and pour over enough boiling water to

cover the wheat. Allow it to cool, by which time the water will be absorbed, and then mix in the oil, diced pepper and pomegranate seeds and season to taste. Just before serving add the mint leaves and mix into the salad.

Preparation time: 20 minutes

MANGE-TOUT AND PEA SALAD

Serves 6

450 g (1 lb) shelled or frozen petits pois
225 g (½ lb) mange-tout
pinch of sugar
150 ml (¼ pint) olive oil
sprig of mint, finely chopped
salt and black pepper

Mange-tout make a wonderful salad. But don't overdo the blanching – they must keep their lovely crispness. As they're often expensive, this recipe cleverly 'pads them out' with ordinary peas.

Trim and blanch the mange-tout, then refresh under cold running water to preserve the

colour. Use the same water to blanch the peas, adding a little sugar to it.
  Mix the remaining ingredients together and pour over the peas. Leave the salad to cool before serving.

Preparation time: 20 minutes

GREEN PEA AND GINGER SALAD

Illustrated on page 31

Serves 6

450 g (1 lb) frozen peas
40 g (1½ oz) spring onions
2 stems ginger
1 tablespoon stem ginger syrup
1 tablespoon white wine vinegar
3 tablespoons light oil
salt and black pepper

An excellent salad for young or frozen peas: ginger and spring onion give a unique flavour.

Cook the frozen peas in boiling salted water, drain and refresh under cold running water. Transfer to a bowl. Chop the spring onions and stem ginger and add them to the peas. Next add the ginger syrup, vinegar and oil. Mix the ingredients well, season with salt and

black pepper and mix again. Cover the salad with clingfilm and refrigerate. Transfer to a dish when you are ready to serve.

Preparation time: 15 minutes

PUDDINGS

RASPBERRY ICE-CREAM

Serves 6

Serves 6

1 × 330 g (12 oz) jar pure
raspberry fruit spread, or
home-made raspberry
purée
2 × 425 g (15 oz) low-fat
yoghurt
50 g (2 oz) caster sugar
fresh raspberries and mint
leaves to garnish

A reasonably healthy, extremely easy-to-make and very popular ice-cream. Use a runny, low-fat yoghurt rather than a thick one and it will have a lovely texture.

Heat the raspberry purée, and push it through a sieve, to remove the pips. Add the yoghurt and sugar and mix well. Transfer the mixture to a plastic container and place in the freezer. When it has begun to set – about 2.5 cm (1 in) around the edges – remove, and stir with a fork (approximately every 2 hours), then return to the freezer. Repeat this twice more and leave to freeze.

An hour or so before serving, transfer the ice-cream from the freezer to the refrigerator, so that it softens a little.

Serve the ice-cream in glasses, and decorate with mint leaves, or another seasonal garnish.

Preparation time: 5 minutes
Freezing time: at least 8 hours

CRANBERRY AND PORT SORBET

Illustrated on page 24

Serves 6

450 g (1 lb) cranberries
2 tablespoons port
225 g (½ lb) granulated
sugar
300 ml (½ pint) water
1 egg white

Both the sweet sorbets in this book are alcoholic, sophisticated and delicious. This one also has the most marvellous colour.

Put the granulated sugar into a saucepan with the water. Bring to a boil, stirring gently as the sugar dissolves, and simmer for 5 minutes. Wash the cranberries and add them to the syrup. Cook for a further 6–10 minutes, or until they start to pop, then pass the cranberry syrup through a sieve. When the mixture is cold, add the port and transfer to a freezer-proof container. Freeze for about 2 hours, or until the sorbet is frozen about 2.5 cm (1 in) around the edge. Remove from the freezer and whisk with a fork. Freeze again until the sorbet has set to a firm slush. Remove from the freezer and beat. Whisk the egg white until stiff but not dry, and fold into the sorbet mixture. Return the sorbet to the freezer overnight.

One hour before serving, transfer the sorbet to the fridge so that it softens a little.

Advance preparation: To taste their best, sorbets should only be kept for a few days.
Preparation time: 25 minutes
Freezing time: 12 hours

CHAMPAGNE SORBET

Illustrated on page 24

Serves 6

600 ml (1 pint) champagne
225 ml (8 fl oz) water
275 g (10 oz) granulated
sugar
3 tablespoons lemon juice
1 egg white

Note: *To make a really smooth sorbet, it is important to beat the semi-frozen mixture well, before adding the egg white.*

You really do need champagne for this very special sorbet: a sparkling white wine just isn't the same.

Put the granulated sugar into a saucepan with 225 ml (8 fl oz) cold water. Bring slowly to a boil, stirring gently as the sugar dissolves. Simmer for 5 minutes, remove from the heat and allow to cool.

When the syrup is cold, add the champagne and lemon juice. Mix and transfer to a freezer-proof container. Freeze for about 2 hours, or until the sorbet is frozen about 2.5 cm (1 in) around the edge. Whisk with a fork and freeze again until it becomes a firm slush. Whisk the egg white until stiff but not dry, then fold it into the champagne mixture and freeze for at least 12 hours.

As this is a soft sorbet, you should be able to serve it straight from the freezer. Spoon it into champagne (or white wine) glasses and serve immediately.

Preparation time: 15 minutes
Freezing time: 12–14 hours

AMARETTO MOUSSE

Serves 6

3 tablespoons Amaretto
  liqueur
120 g (4 oz) Amaretti
  biscuits (and some for
  decoration)
15 g (½ oz) gelatine
4 eggs
85 g (3 oz) light muscavado
300 ml (½ pint) double
  cream
3 teaspoons coffee, or 1
  teaspoon Camp coffee

This is a sophisticated pudding with an intriguing mixture of textures as the biscuits stay crunchy. The liqueur enhances the wonderful almond taste.

Dissolve the gelatine, following the manufacturer's instructions. Meanwhile, separate the eggs into two large bowls and whisk the yolks, with the sieved sugar, until well creamed. Allow the dissolved gelatine to cool a little, then pour it onto the creamed eggs, whisking continuously. Add the Amaretto liqueur and whisk again. Whisk the cream until it holds a peak and fold it, with a few drops of the coffee, into the mixture.

Break up the biscuits with your hands, so that they are still in chunky pieces, and fold them into the mousse. Whisk the egg whites until they stand in stiff peaks and fold into the mousse. Transfer to a serving dish and chill in the fridge until set. To serve, decorate with some whole Amaretti biscuits.

Preparation and cooking time: 25 minutes
Setting time: 2–3 hours

WHITE CHOCOLATE MOUSSE WITH DARK CHOCOLATE SAUCE

Illustrated on page 24

Serves 6

150 g (5 oz) white
  chocolate, grated
175 g (6 oz) plain chocolate
300 ml (½ pint) double
  cream
15 g (½ oz) caster sugar
2 egg whites
75 ml (3 fl oz) water

Wonderfully rich and wicked, it looks good served in ramekins or glasses, like Irish coffee in reverse.

Melt the white chocolate in a bowl, set over a saucepan of hot water. Meanwhile whisk the double cream to a soft peak. When the chocolate has melted, add it to the cream and fold in quickly and lightly with a rubber spatula. Add the sugar and fold again. In a separate bowl, whisk the egg whites to a peak and fold into the chocolate with a metal spoon, a third at a time, until the mixture is smooth. Spoon into glasses and refrigerate.

Melt the plain chocolate in a pan with 75 ml (3 fl oz) water, stirring occasionally. Remove from the heat and allow to cool, then spoon over the white chocolate mousse.

Advance preparation: Make the mousse in advance and refrigerate. The sauce can also be made ahead and added cold when the mousse has set.
Preparation time: 25 minutes
Setting time: 2–3 hours

LEMON SOUFFLÉ

Illustrated on page 63

Serves 6

juice and zest of 4 lemons
oil for greasing
4 eggs, separated
150 g (5 oz) caster sugar
4 teaspoons gelatine
4 tablespoons cold water
300 ml (½ pint) double
  cream
150 g (5 oz) toasted
  almonds, chopped
whipped or double cream,
  to serve

A classic, light but delicious pudding – particularly easy with this method. Very good with Vienna biscuits (page 134) or Hazelnut shortbread (page 135) or, to be extra special, serve it with a sauce made from sieved fresh or frozen raspberries and a little icing sugar.

Make a collar of greaseproof paper to go round a 900 ml (1½ pint) soufflé dish so it stands at least 5 cm (2 in) above the rim. Brush the top part of the collar with oil.

Beat the egg yolks, sugar, lemon zest and juice over a pan of boiling water until thick and creamy. Dissolve the gelatine in the cold water, according to the manufacturer's instructions, and allow to cool slightly before stirring into the lemon mixture. Refrigerate.

Meanwhile, beat the double cream until it just holds its peak – it should be the consistency of the lemon mixture – and fold into the lemon. Whisk the egg whites and fold carefully into the lemon when it has almost set. Pour the mixture into the soufflé mould – it should come above the rim, held in by the greaseproof paper – and chill until set.

When the soufflé has set, release the collar by running a warm knife between the paper and the soufflé. Using a palette knife, stick the almonds around the edge of the soufflé and chill again. Take the soufflé out of the fridge at least 30 minutes before serving to obtain the fullest lemon flavour. Serve with whipped or thick double cream.

Preparation time: 20 minutes
Setting time: 8 hours, or overnight

LIME AND ORANGE SYLLABUB

Illustrated on page 29

Serves 6

300 ml (½ pint) double
   cream
300 ml (½ pint) low-fat
   yoghurt
1 lime
rind of ½ orange
1 tablespoon orange juice
15 g (½ oz) sugar

Topping (optional)
1 tablespoon muesli
1 tablespoon demerara
   sugar

A mixture of yoghurt and cream makes this syllabub particularly light. Serve it in bought chocolate shells, with or without a topping.

Whip the double cream until it holds its shape, then fold in the yoghurt. Add the grated lime and orange peel, together with the lime juice, orange juice and sugar and fold this into the cream. Spoon the mixture into glasses (or ramekin dishes if you are doing a cooked topping) and chill in the refrigerator for at least 12 hours.

For the topping, mix the muesli and sugar together and sprinkle some onto each ramekin dish. Place under a hot grill for a couple of minutes, or until the sugar has melted. Allow to cool before chilling.

Advance preparation: The syllabub can be eaten within two hours of making, but the flavour of the fruits will be more pronounced if you leave it for longer.
Preparation and cooking time: 20 minutes
Chilling time: 12 hours

PAVLOVA

Illustrated on page 31

Serves 6

6 egg whites
340 g (12 oz) caster sugar
melted butter for greasing
1 tablespoon cornflour
   (plus a little for the tin)
1 tablespoon white wine
   vinegar
20.3 cm (8 in) square
   baking tin
300 ml (½ pint) double
   cream
fruits to fill

As this pudding originated in Australia, the fruits generally used are passion fruit and kiwi, but there's no reason why you shouldn't experiment with others. Remember, though, that they should be on the tart side to counteract the sweet meringue.

Heat the oven to 300°F (160°C, gas mark 2). Whisk the egg whites to a stiff peak and fold in the caster sugar, a tablespoon at a time. Whisk continuously, counting to 10 between each tablespoon, so that you don't lose too much air from the meringue. Sift the cornflour into the mixture and fold in with a metal spoon. Finally, add the white wine vinegar and fold again. Line the base of the baking tin with greaseproof paper, brush the paper and sides

with melted butter and sprinkle with cornflour. Spoon the mixture into the prepared tin and arrange in the shape in which you want the meringue to set. Cook in the preheated oven for 2 hours, or until the outside is firm and the inside is soft. While it is still hot, transfer the pavlova to a serving dish. When it cools, the middle will subside. Set aside until ready to decorate.

A few hours before serving, whisk the cream until it holds its peak and spoon it into the centre of the meringue. Decorate with the fruit of your choice.

Preparation time: 15 minutes
Cooking time: 2 hours

APPLE TOPSY-TURVY

Illustrated on page 19

Serves 6

900 g (2 lb) dessert apples,
   peeled, cored and thinly
   sliced
1 tablespoon melted butter
120 g (4 oz) soft brown
   sugar
1 teaspoon ground allspice
   (or cinnamon and
   nutmeg)
50 g (2 oz) currants,
   sultanas or raisins
30 g (1 oz) flaked almonds

This light and delicious pudding is made a bit like a tarte tatin (which is traditionally cooked upside-down), but without the pastry. The apples keep their shape beautifully when the tart is turned out, and if you made it in a heart-shaped tin it would look particularly effective. Make sure you let it cool completely before attempting to turn it out. You could experiment with other kinds of fruit such as pears or peaches.

Heat the oven to 350°F (180°C, gas mark 4). Brush a 20.3 cm (8-in) diameter solid-bottomed cake tin with melted butter, line with greaseproof paper and brush the paper with a little more melted butter.

Cover the base of the tin with sugar and sprinkle over half the spices. Arrange half the apples evenly in the tin and press down. Sprinkle over the dried fruit and nuts and the remaining spices and cover with the remaining apple in another layer. Cover with greaseproof paper and press down again. Bake in the preheated oven for 1½ hours. The tart can be served warm or cool. Turn it out upside down so that the caramel is on top.

Advance preparation: The tart can be reheated in the oven, before serving.
Preparation time: 15 minutes
Cooking time: 1½ hours

FRUIT CLAFOUTIS

Illustrated on page 18

Serves 6

400 g (14 oz) tin pitted
  black cherries
225 g (8 oz) tin apricots
3 eggs
120 g (4 oz) caster sugar
50 g (2 oz) flour
300 ml (½ pint) milk
150 ml (¼ pint) double
  cream
icing sugar to serve

You can make this as sophisticated or as simple as you choose, depending on the fruit you put into it. It would be excellent with fresh peaches, mangoes or grapes, or as a plainer but equally good family dish with apples or pears.

Heat the oven to 375°F (150°C, gas mark 5). Drain the cherries and apricots and place them in an ovenproof dish.

Whisk the eggs and caster sugar in a bowl until light and fluffy, then sift in the flour and whisk again until the mixture is smooth.

Gradually whisk in the milk and cream. Pour this batter over the fruit and cook in the preheated oven for 45 minutes or until it is just set and the top is golden brown. You can serve immediately, or keep it warm in a low oven until ready to serve. Immediately before serving, sprinkle the top with sieved icing sugar. It is also delicious cold.

Preparation time: 10 minutes
Cooking time: 45 minutes

PANCAKE-WRAPPED PEACHES

Illustrated on page 24

Makes 12

For the pancakes
120 g (4 oz) plain flour
salt
3 eggs
300 ml (½ pint) milk
2 tablespoons butter,
  melted
vegetable oil, for cooking

For the filling
6 peaches
120 g (4 oz) granulated
  sugar
450 ml (¾ pint) water
30–50 g (1–2 oz) caster
  sugar
2 tablespoons apricot
  brandy
icing sugar to serve

These look and taste marvellous. If you bought ready-made pancakes, it would be very quick to assemble, but home-made pancakes are so good that it's worth preparing a couple of batches and freezing them.

To make the pancake batter, sift the flour into a food processor or blender, add the salt and eggs and blend. Add the milk and melted butter and blend again (do not overwork or the pancakes will be tough). Leave the batter to stand for 1 hour.

Put in just enough oil to grease the crêpe pan and heat it. Make sure that the oil is very hot before you pour in the batter, and add more lard or butter as necessary. When one side of the pancake is golden – about 1 minute – flip it with a palette knife and cook the other side until golden. Turn out onto greaseproof paper.

To make the filling, dissolve the sugar in the water, then boil for 2 minutes to make a syrup. Reduce the heat until the liquid is just simmering, add the peaches and poach, uncovered, until they are tender but not soft – about 5–6 minutes.

Strain the peaches, reserving the juice. Holding each peach in a clean tea towel so that you don't burn your hand, peel off the skin with a sharp knife. Cut each peach in half and remove the stones.

Place half a peach, cut side up, towards the edge of each pancake. Fold in the sides and wrap the peaches. Continue until you have 12 half peaches wrapped in pancakes.

Cut 24 strips 0.6 cm (¼ in) wide – from the remaining pancakes. Make a loose knot in the centre of 12 strips, and then wrap a straight strip around the centre of each peach. Wrap a knotted strip around the peach in the opposite direction and tuck any loose ends underneath. This will give the effect of a tied-and-knotted parcel. Place the wrapped peaches on a baking tray or flameproof dish.

Sprinkle the pancakes with caster sugar and warm them under a hot grill for 2–3 minutes. Meanwhile warm the fruit syrup, add the apricot brandy and transfer to a sauceboat. Sprinkle the pancakes with icing sugar and transfer them to serving plates.

Advance preparation: The pancakes can be made, and the peaches cooked, the day before. The peaches can be wrapped in the pancakes in the morning. Pancakes can be stored in the fridge for a week, or in the freezer for a couple of months.
Preparation and cooking time: 1½ hours

QUICK FRUIT TART

Illustrated on page 63

Serves 6

300 g (1ˡ oz) plain
    chocolate wholemeal
    biscuits
fresh fruit in season
120 g (4 oz) unsalted butter
50 g (2 oz) chopped mixed
    nuts
225 g (½ pint) crème fraîche
    or whipped cream
100 g (4 oz) caster sugar
3 tablespoons water

This is very quick to do, but if you take a little trouble arranging the fruit in concentric circles or radiating stripes it will look magnificent. Choose fruits of contrasting colours.

Put the biscuits into a polythene bag and crush them with a rolling pin. Melt the butter in a saucepan, remove from the heat and add the biscuits and the nuts. Press the mixture into a round 25.5 cm (10 in) flan dish – preferably one with a loose base – and allow it to cool.
    Spread the biscuit base with the crème fraîche (or cream) and arrange a variety of whole or sliced fresh fruit on top of it. If you want to serve the cream separately, brush the biscuit base with egg white, allow it to dry and then arrange the fruit.
    In a thick-bottomed pan dissolve the sugar in the water by boiling rapidly for 3 minutes without stirring. Dribble this syrup over the fruit and allow it to set before serving.

Preparation and cooking time: 30 minutes

STUFFED PEARS WITH CHOCOLATE SAUCE

Illustrated on page 12

Serves 6

6 ripe thin-skinned pears,
    such as Williams
50 g (2 oz) hazelnuts,
    shelled and skinned
lemon juice

For the sauce
170 g (6 oz) plain chocolate
6 tablespoons water
100 g (4 oz) caster sugar
6 tablespoons orange juice
25 g (1 oz) hazelnuts,
    shelled and skinned

This is a fabulous pudding – with or without the chocolate sauce. The hazelnuts and orange juice give the pears a magnificent flavour. Decorate the chilled pears with mint leaves or freesia flowers and serve with whipped cream as well as the chocolate sauce.

Cut the base off each pear, so that it is flat, and scoop out the core with a teaspoon. Coarsely chop the hazelnuts, by hand or in a food processor. Brush the inside of the pears with lemon juice and balance each pear upside down in a glass so that the nuts don't fall out while you spoon in the hazelnut filling. Place the pears on a dish in the fridge for 2–3 hours or overnight.
    For the sauce, place the water and sugar in a pan and heat until sugar dissolves. Add the orange juice and grated chocolate and stir over a gentle heat until the chocolate has dissolved. Add chopped hazelnuts for a more crunchy texture, and keep the sauce warm until you are ready to serve it.

Preparation time: 25 minutes
Chilling time: 2–3 hours

SPICY APPLE MERINGUE

Illustrated on page 19

Serves 6

1.4 kg (3 lb) cooking
    apples, peeled, cored and
    sliced
3 eggs, separated
½ teaspoon nutmeg
½ teaspoon cinnamon
3 cloves
200 g (7 oz) caster sugar
4 tablespoons lemon juice
pinch of salt
30 g (1 oz) almonds,
    blanched and halved

This is a wonderful mixture of spicy apple purée with a crunchy almond and meringue topping.

Heat the oven to 375°F (190°C, gas mark 5). Butter an ovenproof dish and place the sliced apples in it. Sprinkle spices and 30 g (1 oz) sugar over the top and pour on the lemon juice. Cover the dish with foil and bake for 30 minutes in the preheated oven.
    Remove the dish from the oven and mash the apples with a fork (or process in a food processor if you want a really smooth purée), then beat in the egg yolks.
    Whisk the egg whites with the salt until they form soft peaks, then tip in 85 g (3 oz) sugar and continue to whisk until the egg is stiff. Fold in the rest of the sugar with a metal spoon and spread the meringue mixture over the apple. Push the almonds into the uncooked meringue so that they are half visible, and bake in a very cool oven – 275°F (140°C, gas mark 1) – for about 1 hour. Serve straight from the oven, or cool to room temperature.

Preparation time: 45 minutes
Cooking time: 1 hour

APPLE SQUARE PUFFS

Illustrated on page 86

Serves 6

3 dessert apples
1 × 320 g (11.6 oz) packet
   frozen puff pastry,
   defrosted
1 egg yolk
3 tablespoons caster sugar
1½ teaspoons cinnamon
   powder

A beautifully simple idea and yet very showy, you could stuff the apple with dried fruit or nuts. Try it with pears too.

Heat the oven to 400°F (200°C, gas mark 6). Roll the pastry on a floured surface and cut 6 squares large enough to hold half an apple. Reserve the pastry trimmings. Sprinkle water on a baking tray and place the pastry squares on it. Brush with water and egg yolk.

Combine the sugar and cinnamon in a small dish. Peel the apples, cut them in half and coat the outside in cinnamon and sugar. Place half an apple on each square, cut-side down.

Roll out the pastry trimmings, cut 12 'leaves' and place two below each apple. Brush with egg yolk and cook in the oven for 20 minutes or until the pastry is crisp and golden.

Preparation and cooking time: 30 minutes

PUMPKIN PIE

Illustrated on page 64

Serves 8

25.5 cm (10 in) pastry case,
   baked blind
450 g (1 lb) pumpkin purée
3 eggs
85 g (3 oz) soft brown sugar
½ teaspoon ground
   cinnamon
½ teaspoon ground ginger
½ teaspoon nutmeg
½ teaspoon mace
300 ml (½ pint) double
   cream

Do try this: I never much liked pumpkin pie before I tried this version, and of course it's another way of using up the flesh from your Hallowe'en lantern. You can use tinned pumpkin purée, but home-made tastes much better and has a smoother texture. Serve with a tart apple purée rather than cream, which would be too rich.

If you make it for Hallowe'en, it's fun to decorate it with a spider's web (melted chocolate or black-coloured icing in a piping bag) with its own spider (made from a cake rolled in chocolate vermicelli with liquorice or angelica legs).

Heat the oven to 350°F (180°C, gas mark 4). Place the pumpkin purée in a bowl and whisk in the eggs, one at a time. Add the soft brown sugar and the spices. In a separate bowl whisk the cream and fold it into the pumpkin mixture with a large metal spoon. Pour the mixture into the pastry case and cook in a tart tin in the oven for 30 minutes, until firm. When cooked, remove from the tin. Serve hot or cold.

Preparation time: 10 minutes
Cooking time: 30 minutes

PLUM CRUMBLE

Illustrated on page 18

Serves 6

1.3 kg (3 lb) ripe red plums
225 g (½ lb) dried peaches,
   coarsely chopped
150 ml (¼ pint) orange juice
120 g (4 oz) soft dark
   brown sugar
120 g (4 oz) self-raising
   wholemeal flour
120 g (2 oz) flaked almonds
85 g (3 oz) butter

I love crumble: one of the great English puddings. You can make it with almost any fruit or in different combinations, but this version adds nuts to the topping and dried fruit to the fresh.

Heat the oven to 350°F (180°C, gas mark 4). Coarsely chop the dried peaches and place in a bowl. Heat the orange juice and pour over the peaches. Stone and quarter the plums and put half of them into a 1.8 litre (3 pint) soufflé dish,

plus half the peaches and half the orange juice. Sprinkle over 30 g (1 oz) brown sugar, add the remaining plums, peaches and juice and sprinkle over 30 g (1 oz) brown sugar.

Rub together the dry ingredients, butter and remaining sugar and sprinkle over fruit. Cook in the preheated oven for 30 minutes.

Preparation time: 15 minutes
Cooking time: 30 minutes

CRÈME ANGLAISE

Makes 600 ml (1 pint)

600 ml (1 pint) milk
1 vanilla pod
4 egg yolks
3–4 tablespoons sugar
1 teaspoon sugar, for
   sprinkling

(Or real custard as I would call it!) Not just an alternative to cream but great for all cooked fruit.

Bring the milk to a boil with the vanilla pod, remove from the heat and infuse for 10 minutes. Beat the yolks and sugar until light and creamy, remove the vanilla pod and

slowly pour on the milk, stirring constantly. Strain the sauce back into the pan and stir over a gentle heat until it is the consistency of double cream. Sprinkle with sugar to prevent a skin forming. Serve hot or cold.

Preparation and cooking time: 25 minutes

BISCUITS AND CAKES

BLUEBERRY MUFFINS

Illustrated on page 39

Makes 12

425 g (15 oz) tin
    blueberries, strained
3 tablespoons corn oil
1 egg
175 g (6 oz) milk
120 g (4 oz) butter
250 g (9 oz) plain flour
3 tablespoons caster sugar
2 teaspoons baking powder
pinch of salt

American muffins don't resemble the English ones we eat toasted with butter. They are like large cupcakes, though less sweet and more wholesome. I adore them – for brunch or tea – and with blueberries they are unbeatable. Try blackcurrants if you can't find blueberries.

Heat the oven to 400°F (200°C, gas mark 6). Grease the 7 cm (2¾ in) diameter muffin tins with 1 tablespoon of oil.
    Beat the egg in a bowl, stir in the milk and remaining oil. Mix in the butter and all the dry ingredients until the flour is absorbed, but still lumpy. Now fold in the strained blueberries and mix well. Fill the muffin tins two thirds full with the mixture.
    Cook in the preheated oven for 20–25 minutes, or until the muffins have risen and come away from the sides.

Preparation time: 10 minutes
Cooking time: 20–25 minutes

CINNAMON HEARTS

Illustrated on page 35

Makes about 24

225 g (½ lb) butter
50 g (2 oz) lard
175 g (6 oz) caster sugar
340 g (¾ lb) plain flour
1 teaspoon cinnamon

Note: *Make sure you have a baking tray which will fit into the fridge.*

These are crisp biscuits which would go well with ice-cream or cooked fruit as a pudding. They'd also be lovely hung on the tree at Christmas time.

Put the butter, lard and sugar into a food processor or blender and blend until smooth. Add the flour and cinnamon and blend until the mixture starts to come together, but be careful not to overwork it as it will become tough. Form the mixture into a ball, wrap it in clingfilm and chill in the fridge for approximately 5 hours.
    Sprinkle the work surface with a little flour, remove the dough from the fridge and roll it to just over 1.2 cm (½ in) thick. Using a heart-shaped cutter, cut the biscuits from the dough and transfer them to an ungreased baking sheet. Place in the fridge for about 45 minutes.
    Heat the oven to 325°F (170°C, gas mark 3). Pierce each biscuit with a skewer to make a hole in the centre (or use a tiny heart-shaped cutter). Bake in the preheated oven for 20 minutes, or until they just start to colour. When the biscuits are cooked, remove from the oven. Pierce each hole again with the skewer and transfer to a baking rack to cool. When the biscuits are ready, thread a ribbon through each one and hang as desired.

Preparation and chilling time: 5–6 hours
Cooking time: 20 minutes

VIENNA BISCUITS

Illustrated on page 51

Makes about 18

85 g (3 oz) butter, softened
25 g (1 oz) icing sugar
150 g (5 oz) plain flour

For chocolate coating
225 g (8 oz) plain chocolate
vegetable oil

My favourite biscuits – terribly simple, but served with a syllabub or fruit fool, they are wonderful. If the butter is soft enough, you can pipe the mixture instead of rolling it into balls, and make pretty shell patterns, or long fingers. These can be dipped into melted chocolate for a party-time treat.

Heat the oven to 375°F (190°C, gas mark 5). Combine the ingredients in a bowl and blend together until smooth. With well-floured hands roll teaspoonfuls of the mixture into balls. Press each one onto a greased baking tray with the bottom of a cut-glass tumbler to make a pretty pattern on each biscuit. Bake in the preheated oven for 10–15 minutes, until just beginning to colour. Remove from the oven and leave to cool on a cake rack.
    For the chocolate coating, break the chocolate into a bowl and melt it over a pan of hot water (if necessary, add a little vegetable oil to achieve the right coating consistency). Dip the biscuits into the chocolate and place on parchment paper until the chocolate has hardened.

Preparation time: 10 minutes
Cooking time: 15 minutes

HAZELNUT SHORTBREAD

Illustrated on page 47

Makes about 24

120 g (4 oz) butter, softened
120 g (4 oz) caster sugar
1 egg yolk
120 g (4 oz) plain flour
pinch of salt
50 g (2 oz) ground hazelnuts

Shortbread originated in Scotland, which has some of the best bakeries in the world. It is always popular, and in this recipe the added hazelnuts give it a special flavour. You could make it into a circle, and mark with a sharp knife into the traditional 'petticoat tails' instead of baking it in pieces.

Heat the oven to 325°F (150°C, gas mark 3). Cream the butter and sugar until light and fluffy. Add the egg yolk and beat or process the mixture for 1–2 minutes until the egg is absorbed. Mix in the dry ingredients until they are well blended and the mixture has formed a ball. Dust the ball with flour, wrap in polythene and then chill in the fridge for about 1 hour.

Roll the ball out on a floured board to a thickness of about 0.6 cm (¼ in). Cut out whatever shapes you want and arrange them on a greased baking sheet. Bake in the preheated oven for 10–15 minutes until golden brown, then remove from the oven and cool on a wire rack. Store in an airtight tin.

Preparation time: 25 minutes
Cooking time: 10–15 minutes

FIG FINGERS

Illustrated on page 47

Makes 12

225 g (½ lb) dried figs
225 g (½ lb) stoned prunes
120 g (4 oz) porridge oats
120 g (4 oz) butter, softened
120 g (4 oz) plain flour
50 g (2 oz) soft brown sugar
½ teaspoon bicarbonate of soda

Note: *If you don't have a non-stick cake tin, line one with greaseproof paper.*

These are popular with young and old. Once you've cooked the fruit the children could help you make them. They're perfect for picnics.

Heat the oven to 350°F (180°C, gas mark 4). Remove the stalks from the figs and place them in a saucepan with the stoned prunes. Cover with cold water, bring to a boil and simmer for 20–30 minutes, until the fruit is soft. Drain and blend in a food processor or blender. Place the remaining ingredients in a bowl and mix together.

Place half of the oat mixture in a 17.8 cm (7 in) square tin and spread it over the base. Spread the fig and prune mixture on top of the oats and add the rest of the oat mixture. Bake in the preheated oven for 30 minutes, or until the oats are lightly browned. Allow to cool in the tin before turning out onto a baking tray. When the oat biscuit is cool, cut it into fingers for serving.

Preparation time: 40 minutes
Cooking time: 30 minutes

BANANA CAKE WITH PEACHES AND PEARS

Illustrated on page 47

Serves 12

340 g (12 oz) bananas
85 g (3 oz) dried peaches, coarsely chopped
85 g (3 oz) dried pears, coarsely chopped
225 g (½ lb) butter
225 g (½ lb) caster sugar
3 eggs
225 g (½ lb) plain flour
½ teaspoon salt
¼ teaspoon bicarbonate of soda
3 tablespoons yoghurt
butter and flour for cake tin

This wonderful-tasting, firm cake is also reasonably 'healthy' and can be served on many different occasions. Leave it plain, dust it with a little icing sugar or perhaps even ice it properly. It would also be delicious spread with a little Crème Anglaise (page 133) and decorated with pieces of dried fruit.

Heat the oven to 350°F (180°C, gas mark 4). Butter and flour a 20.3 cm (8 in) square cake tin. Cream the butter and sugar together in a bowl, then add the eggs, one at a time, beating well. Blend the bananas and whisk into the mixture in the bowl. Sift the dry ingredients (flour, salt and bicarbonate of soda) and fold in with a metal spoon. Add the yoghurt and the chopped dried fruits and fold in well. Pour the mixture into the cake tin and bake in the preheated oven for 1 hour, or until a skewer comes out clean when inserted.

Leave the cake to cool in the tin for 10 minutes, then run a knife around the edge and turn the cake out onto a rack to cool completely before serving.

Preparation time: 15 minutes
Cooking time: 1 hour
Cooling time: 10 minutes

NUT CAKE

Serves 6–8

100 g (3½ oz) caster sugar
100 g (3½ oz) unsalted butter, at room temperature
2 eggs (size 2)
1 teaspoon ground cinnamon
2 tablespoons brandy
100 g (3½ oz) shelled walnuts, chopped
100 g (3½ oz) shelled pecan nuts, chopped
50 g (2 oz) pine nuts
200 g (7 oz) plain flour
½ teaspoon baking powder

Made with walnuts, pecan nuts and pine nuts, and flavoured with cinnamon and brandy, this is a cake that will keep quite well. Of course, being so good, it's unlikely to last too long. To make a change, serve it as a pudding with stewed fruit.

Heat the oven to 350°F (180°C, gas mark 4). Grease and flour a 23 cm (9 in) round cake tin. Cream together the sugar and butter until light and fluffy. Add the eggs, cinnamon and brandy and beat well to mix.

Stir in the walnuts, pecan nuts and pine nuts. Sift over the flour and baking powder and fold them into the nut mixture.

Pour the mixture into the prepared cake tin. Bake in the preheated oven for 35–45 minutes or until a skewer inserted in the centre of the cake comes out clean. Turn out and leave to cool on a wire rack.

Preparation time: 15 minutes
Cooking time: 35–45 minutes

MINCEMEAT BISCUITS

Makes 20–22

100 g (3½ oz) butter, at room temperature
100 g (3½ oz) dark brown sugar
1 egg (size 2)
175 g (6 oz) plain flour
¼ teaspoon baking powder
½ teaspoon bicarbonate of soda
½ teaspoon ground cinnamon
100 g (3½ oz) rolled oats
200 g (7 oz) mincemeat
100 g (3½ oz) chopped walnuts
For the glaze
200 g (7 oz) icing sugar
¾ teaspoon ground cinnamon
2 tablespoons brandy
3 tablespoons water

Although mince pies and other treats made with mincemeat are most often eaten at Christmas time, these biscuits are too delicious for just a holiday appearance. For plainer biscuits, you can make them without the glaze. Either way, they will be much appreciated by all the family.

Heat the oven to 400°F (200°C, gas mark 6). Cream together the butter and sugar until light and fluffy. Beat in the egg. Mix together the plain flour, baking powder, bicarbonate of soda, ground cinnamon and rolled oats. Gradually add to the creamed butter and sugar mixture, beating gently. Then stir in the mincemeat and walnuts.

Place the dough in tablespoonfuls, 7.5 cm (3 in) apart to allow room for spreading, on a greased baking sheet. Bake the biscuits in the preheated oven for 8–10 minutes.

To make the glaze, mix together the sifted icing sugar, cinnamon, brandy and water until smooth. Transfer the hot mincemeat biscuits from the baking sheet to a wire rack and brush them over the top with the glaze. Leave to cool.

Preparation time: 20 minutes
Cooking time: 8–10 minutes

BLACK AND WHITE THINS

Makes 30

25 g (1 oz) plain chocolate
100 g (3½ oz) butter, at room temperature
50 g (2 oz) caster sugar
1 egg yolk
200 g (7 oz) plain flour
1½ teaspoons baking powder
1–2 tablespoons milk

These are elegant biscuits – thin and crisp and wonderfully stripy. Serve them with ice-cream, sorbet or a fresh fruit dessert.

Melt the plain chocolate in a heatproof bowl set over a pan of hot water, or alternatively melt it in the microwave. Set it aside to cool slightly. Cream together the butter and sugar until light and fluffy. Beat in the egg yolk. Sift over the flour and baking powder and beat gently to make a smooth dough, adding the milk as it is needed.

Cut the dough in half and mix the chocolate into one half. Shape each piece of dough into a long roll 4 cm (1½ in) in diameter, wrap in greaseproof paper or cling film and flatten each side to square it.

Refrigerate for at least 3 hours or up to 24 hours.

Heat the oven to 350°F (180°C, gas mark 4). Remove the paper or cling film from the dough. Cut each block of dough into four lengthways. Take two white and two dark pieces and reassemble the two blocks in stripes. Gently press together to seal. Cut across into 5 mm (¼ in) slices and lay them 2.5 cm (1 in) apart on a greased baking sheet.

Bake the biscuits in the preheated oven for 7–10 minutes or until they are golden brown. Transfer them to a wire rack and allow to cool. Store in an airtight tin.

Preparation time: 20 minutes plus chilling
Cooking time: 7–10 minutes

CHOCOLATE ALMOND CAKE

Serves 6–8

cocoa powder for the tin
150 g (5 oz) bitter chocolate, chopped
1 teaspoon instant coffee powder
4 tablespoons water
175 g (6 oz) butter, at room temperature
175 g (6 oz) caster sugar
5 eggs, separated
200 g (7 oz) chopped almonds
50 g (2 oz) wholemeal breadcrumbs
1 tablespoon icing sugar
300 ml (½ pint) double cream

A chocoholic's delight. This moist cake is made with bitter chocolate and it uses almonds and breadcrumbs instead of flour.

Heat the oven to 325°F (170°C, gas mark 3). Grease a loose-bottomed 25 cm (10 in) cake tin with butter and dust with cocoa powder. Place the chopped chocolate, coffee powder and water in a heatproof bowl and set over a pan of hot water. Stir until melted and smooth. Alternatively, melt these ingredients in the microwave. Set aside to cool slightly.

Cream together the butter and sugar until light and fluffy. Beat in the egg yolks one at a time. Beat in the chocolate mixture, chopped almonds and breadcrumbs. Whisk the egg whites to a stiff peak and fold them into the chocolate mixture. Turn the mixture into the prepared cake tin and gently spread out evenly.

Bake in the preheated oven for 45 minutes–1 hour or until a crust has formed on the top of the cake and the centre feels set. Cool on a wire rack. Before serving, sprinkle with sifted icing sugar. Serve the chocolate almond cake with double cream.

Preparation time: 20 minutes
Cooking time: 45 minutes–1 hour

CHOCOLATE KISSES

Makes 30

175 g (6 oz) plain chocolate, chopped
100 g (3½ oz) butter, at room temperature
150 g (5 oz) caster sugar
2 eggs
200 g (7 oz) plain flour
½ teaspoon baking powder
½ teaspoon bicarbonate of soda

For these delicious little biscuits, the chocolate dough is shaped into balls and rolled in sugar before baking. Use a good-quality plain chocolate, such as a chocolat pâtissier, for best results. You'll be asked to make them again and again.

Heat the oven to 350°F (180°C, gas mark 4). Melt the plain chocolate in a heatproof bowl set in a pan of hot water. Alternatively, melt it in the microwave. Set the melted chocolate aside to cool slightly. Cream together the butter and 100 g (3½ oz) of the sugar until light and fluffy. Beat in the eggs, one at a time, and the melted chocolate. Then sift in the plain flour, baking powder and bicarbonate of soda and mix together thoroughly. Chill the dough for 1 hour.

Put the remaining sugar in a bowl. Shape the dough into 2.5 cm (1 in) balls and coat them with the sugar. Arrange on a baking sheet and bake in the preheated oven for 12–15 minutes or until the coating seems dry. Transfer to a wire rack and allow to cool. Store in an airtight tin.

Preparation time: 15 minutes
Chilling time: 1 hour
Cooking time: 12–15 minutes

COURGETTE BISCUITS

Makes 30

100 g (3½ oz) unsalted butter, at room temperature
100 g (3½ oz) caster sugar
1 egg (size 2), beaten
85 g (3 oz) courgette, grated
200 g (7 oz) plain flour
1 teaspoon bicarbonate of soda
½ teaspoon ground cinnamon
½ teaspoon salt
50 g (2 oz) raisins
85 g (3 oz) shelled walnuts, chopped

You might think these unusual biscuits are savoury, as they contain grated courgette, but in fact they are deliciously sweet and spicy. Raisins and chopped walnuts are added too. With all these wholesome ingredients, these biscuits are perfect to add to a child's lunch box or to take on a picnic.

Heat the oven to 350°F (180°C, gas mark 4). Cream together the unsalted butter and sugar until light and fluffy. Beat in the egg. Stir in the grated courgette. Then sift the plain flour, cinnamon and salt into the mixture and stir in together with the raisins and chopped walnuts.

Drop the mixture in heaped teaspoonfuls onto baking sheets, keeping them 5 cm (2 in) apart to allow for spreading. Bake in the preheated oven for 10 minutes, or until the edges are golden and the biscuits are firm to the touch. Transfer the biscuits with a metal spatula to a wire rack and allow them to cool. These biscuits can be stored in an airtight tin for up to 3 days.

Preparation time: 25 minutes
Cooking time: 10 minutes

MARINADES, SAUCES AND ACCOMPANIMENTS

MARINADES

Marinating not only adds flavour to meat or fish (or cheese), but if left long enough can tenderize it too. However, don't add salt. Remember to turn the meat or fish to keep all sides coated.

When possible, marinate meat and poultry overnight; fish needs only 30 minutes, but don't marinate at all if it is very oily. If you're short of time, make slits in the meat and keep the marinade at room temperature. Brush the food during cooking so it doesn't dry out.

Red wine marinade is good for red meat, white wine for fish and satay for chicken or pork. Mix the ingredients together and pour over the meat. Marinades for meat are improved by adding herbs – see our suggestions left. Instructions for Tandoori marinade appear on page 111.

Adding herbs
With beef: add basil or oregano
With lamb: add rosemary
With pork: add juniper or thyme

Red Wine Marinade
150 ml (5 fl oz) red wine
150 ml (5 fl oz) olive oil
1 tablespoon dry sherry
2 cloves garlic, crushed
1 small onion, sliced
1 teaspoon black pepper
1 bay leaf

Satay Marinade
50 ml (2 fl oz) sesame oil
75 ml (3 fl oz) peanut oil
1 tablespoon soy sauce
1 tablespoon lemon juice
3 tablespoons fresh ginger, chopped
4 cloves garlic, crushed

White Wine Marinade
150 ml (5 fl oz) white wine
150 ml (5 fl oz) white wine vinegar
150 ml (5 fl oz) sunflower oil
2 shallots, chopped
1 teaspoon tarragon, chopped

BARBECUE SAUCE

Illustrated on page 43

Makes 600 ml (1 pint)

150 ml (¼ pint) tomato ketchup
300 ml (½ pint) olive oil
2 tablespoons Worcester sauce
2 tablespoons honey
2 tablespoons lemon juice

Quick, easy and very good served with barbecued meat, poultry or fish kebabs. You could also spoon a little over the meat while it's barbecueing.

Mix the ingredients together, season to taste and serve.

Advance preparation: You can make this the day before and store in the fridge until needed.
Preparation time: 5 minutes

PEANUT BUTTER SAUCE

Illustrated on page 43

Makes 150 ml (¼ pint)

7 tablespoons peanut butter
1 large onion, chopped
2 tablespoons butter
150 ml (¼ pint) milk
2 tablespoons tomato ketchup
½ teaspoon yeast extract
1 teaspoon Worcester sauce
salt and pepper

This is so popular when served with barbecued meat and poultry that, once the family has tried it, it may become part of your regular repertoire.

Melt the butter in a saucepan and cook the onion until just browned. Add the peanut butter, stirring until it is heated through. Add the milk, still stirring, and then add the ketchup, yeast extract and Worcester sauce. Season to taste.

Cooking time: 5 minutes

LOW-FAT MAYONNAISE

Makes 300 ml (½ pint)

2 egg yolks
2 tablespoons corn oil
400 g (1 lb 2 oz) Greek yoghurt
salt and white pepper

This is an excellent and much healthier alternative to the traditional creamy salad dressing. You can add a tablespoon of any chopped fresh herb; try basil, dill, tarragon, or marjoram.

Put the egg yolks into a bowl and whisk with an electric whisk. Gradually add the oil and then the yoghurt, a tablespoon at a time, and continue beating until the mixture emulsifies and thickens. Season to taste.

Preparation time: 10–15 minutes
Advance preparation: You can store the mayonnaise in the fridge for up to 4 days.

SPICED PLUMS

Illustrated on page 67

Serves 6

900 g (2 lb) Victoria plums
300 ml (½ pint) cider vinegar
85 g (3 oz) soft brown sugar
175 g (6 oz) demerara sugar
1 level tablespoon cornflour
1 tablespoon water

Try making this simple, quick recipe with other fruit too: apricots, cherries, peaches or cranberries. It's good with cold meat and with hot pork or ham.

Remove the stones from the plums and slice them. Put the vinegar and sugars into a pan and bring to a boil. Cook until the sugar has dissolved. Add the sliced plums and simmer for 30 minutes so that they are cooked, but still firm. Remove the fruit from the pan with a slotted spoon. Bring the juice to a boil. Mix a tablespoon of cornflour with a tablespoon of cold water and add this to the boiling liquid. Cook until the liquid has reduced by half. Pour the sauce over the plums and allow to cool. Store the preserved fruit in jars in the fridge until ready to serve.

Advance preparation: This can be made several days in advance.

APRICOT SAUCE

Illustrated on page 41

Makes 300 ml (½ pint)

1 × 430 g (15½ oz) tin apricots
2 tablespoons white wine vinegar
1 tablespoon soft brown sugar
pinch of ground cinnamon
¼ teaspoon grated nutmeg

This delicious, tangy apricot sauce makes a change from redcurrant jelly or mint sauce to serve with grilled or roast lamb. It's worth trying it with all sorts of other cooked meats, too.

Drain the apricots, reserving the juice, and purée until smooth. Add the vinegar, sugar and spices to the apricot purée and heat very gently. Add enough of the apricot juice to give the consistency you like.

Preparation time: 10 minutes

TOMATO SAUCE

Serves 6

1 × 400 g (14 oz) can chopped tomatoes
1 small onion
1½ tablespoons vegetable oil
1 clove garlic
½ teaspoon sugar
175 ml (¼ pint) red wine
½ teaspoon dried oregano
salt and black pepper
1 small bay leaf

Make lots of this hugely versatile sauce and keep some in the freezer. It's wonderful served elegantly with any vegetable dish, or poured over almost anything from hamburgers and sausages to grilled chicken breasts.

Finely chop the onion and cook it in the oil for about 5 minutes. Add the crushed garlic and continue to cook until the onion is soft and transparent. Add the remaining ingredients and simmer for 20 minutes, uncovered, until the sauce is the consistency you require. Remove the bay leaf before serving. If you want a very smooth sauce, purée it briefly after cooking.

Preparation and cooking time: 30 minutes

WATERCRESS SAUCE

Makes 600 ml (1 pint)

1 bunch watercress
4 shallots, chopped
50 g (2 oz) butter
600 ml (1 pint) double cream
2–3 tablespoons chives and fennel or dill, chopped

This is a good sauce to serve with Fish en croûte (page 99) or any hot poached fish and it is a marvellous dark green colour.

Cook the shallots in the butter for 5 minutes or until tender. Trim and chop the watercress, add to the shallots and cook until the watercress wilts. Add the cream and bring to a boil. Allow to cool a little, then liquidize until smooth. When reheating, do not allow the sauce to boil for too long as it will lose its colour. Serve with finely chopped herbs.

Advance preparation: Don't make the sauce more than a couple of hours in advance, as it will lose its colour.
Preparation and cooking time: 20 minutes

CHARMOULA

Serves 6

4–5 cloves garlic, chopped
6–8 tablespoons chopped
fresh coriander leaves
6–8 tablespoons chopped
parsley
2 tablespoons white wine
vinegar
2–3 tablespoons lemon juice
1½ teaspoons salt
1–2 teaspoons paprika
1 teaspoon ground cumin

This piquant mixture of herbs, spices, garlic and lemon juice comes from Morocco. It can be served as an unusual sauce, or used as a marinade for fish. This recipe makes enough marinade for a 2.2 kg (5 lb) fish. Alternatively charmoula can be cooked in an exotic dish such as the Fish tagine with tomato on page 101.

Either with a pestle and mortar, or in a mini chopper, crush the chopped garlic. Add the chopped fresh coriander leaves, the chopped parsley and the vinegar to the garlic and work together to make a paste.

Then add the lemon juice, salt, paprika and ground cumin to the paste, mixing all the ingredients together thoroughly.

Preparation time: 10 minutes

PESTO SAUCE

Serves 4–6

6 tablespoons finely chopped
basil
50 g (2 oz) Parmesan cheese,
freshly grated
3–4 tablespoons olive oil
2–3 tablespoons pine nuts,
finely chopped
salt and black pepper

Pesto is a delicious, aromatic Italian sauce based on basil, pine nuts and Parmesan cheese. If only a few spoonfuls are needed for a recipe, you can use a bought pesto, but to dress pasta, nothing can beat the freshly made sauce.

Mix together the finely chopped basil and the freshly grated Parmesan cheese. Add the olive oil, whisking hard.

Stir in the finely chopped pine nuts, and season to taste with salt and freshly ground black pepper.

Preparation time: 10 minutes

HOT BACON AND CHEDDAR SAUCE

Makes 300 ml (½ pint)

8 rashers streaky bacon
3 tablespoons plain flour
300 ml (½ pint) milk
150 ml (¼ pint) pale ale
1 teaspoon Worcestershire
sauce
tabasco sauce
120 g (4 oz) mature Cheddar
cheese, grated

This spicy cheese and bacon sauce is an adaptation of a traditional Welsh rarebit. Try it on plain vegetables such as steamed cauliflower or broccoli, or alternatively serve it as a party dip with baked potato skins or corn chips.

In a frying pan, cook the bacon until crisp. Place it on a paper towel to drain. Pour off all but 2 tablespoons of bacon fat from the pan. Stir in the flour and cook for 3 minutes, stirring. Add the milk, stirring constantly, and then the beer.

Whisk in the Worcestershire sauce and tabasco sauce to taste and cook for 2 minutes, still stirring, until the sauce is thick and smooth. Add 85 g (3 oz) of the Cheddar and the crumbled bacon and cook over a low heat until the cheese has melted. Use the remaining cheese as a garnish and serve immediately.

Preparation time: 5 minutes
Cooking time: 25 minutes

SMOKED SALMON SAUCE

Makes 450 ml (¾ pint)

225 g (½ lb) ricotta cheese
150 ml (¼ pint) soured cream
1 tablespoon lemon juice
120 g (¼ lb) smoked salmon,
finely chopped
1–2 tablespoons chopped dill
salt and white pepper

This is a luxurious creamy sauce ideal for cold asparagus or hard-boiled eggs. It looks so pretty too – pale pink flecked with specks of fresh dill.

In a food processor, blend together the ricotta cheese, soured cream and lemon juice until smooth. Stir in the finely chopped smoked salmon and the chopped dill until the mixture is well combined, and season to taste with salt and freshly ground pepper.

Preparation time: 10 minutes

BANANA YOGHURT SAUCE

Makes about 450 ml (¾ pint)

2 ripe bananas
1 teaspoon lemon juice
2 × 150 g (5 oz) cartons natural
  yoghurt
½ teaspoon grated orange rind
2-3 tablespoons fresh orange
  juice
1 teaspoon orange-flower
  water

Fresh orange and orange-flower water give an exotic flavour to this refreshing sauce, which is sweetened with banana. Serve it with a fresh fruit salad or with a fruity ice-cream to make a delicious pudding.

Cut the banana into pieces. In a food processor, blend the bananas, lemon juice, yoghurt, grated orange rind, fresh orange juice and orange-flower water until smooth.

Chill the sauce, covered, for about 1 hour, but not for too much longer in case it begins to discolour.

Preparation time: 10 minutes
Chilling time: 1 hour

CHOCOLATE FUDGE SAUCE

Makes 450 ml (¾ pint)

100 g (3½ oz) plain chocolate
50 g (2 oz) unsalted butter
300 ml (½ pint) evaporated
  milk
200 g (7 oz) sugar
½ teaspoon salt

Thick and smooth, this chocolate fudge sauce is quite irresistible. Spoon it over vanilla, chocolate or coffee ice-cream, or try it with a slice of cake such as the Nut cake on page 136.

Chop the chocolate. Place the chocolate and butter in a heatproof bowl and set over a pan of hot water (or use a double saucepan). Heat, stirring occasionally, until melted and smooth.

Add the evaporated milk, sugar and salt and cook the mixture, stirring occasionally, for 20 minutes or until thick and smooth. Transfer to a bowl and chill, covered, overnight.

Preparation time: 10 minutes
Cooking time: 20 minutes plus chilling

ALMOND AND HOT PEPPER SAUCE

Makes 450 ml (¾ pint)

1 red pepper
4 large cloves garlic
2 tablespoons blanched
  almonds, lightly toasted
¼ teaspoon dried hot pepper
  flakes
1 teaspoon lemon juice
1 teaspoon dry sherry
2 large egg yolks
300 ml (½ pint) olive oil
50 g (2 oz) fine fresh
  breadcrumbs
salt and black pepper

Almonds, red pepper, sherry, lots of garlic and dried red chilli are used to flavour this wonderful mayonnaise-like sauce which will add a fiery touch to a meal. Its lively taste and pretty colour make it an excellent accompaniment to plainly cooked fish or fish soups which might otherwise be rather bland. It would also be a good choice to serve with barbequed food.

Skin the red pepper as described on page 85 and remove the seeds. Blanch the garlic cloves for 2 minutes, then drain and peel them. In a food processor, blend the toasted blanched almonds, red pepper, dried hot pepper flakes, garlic, lemon juice and sherry until the mixture forms a paste.

Add the egg yolks and when the ingredients are well blended, add the olive oil in a slow stream with the motor running, blending the mixture until it is emulsified. Finally, add the fresh breadcrumbs and season the sauce with salt and black pepper.

Advance preparation: For convenience, the almond and hot pepper sauce can be made up to 3 days in advance and kept, covered, in the refrigerator.
Preparation time: 30 minutes

INDEX

ACKNOWLEDGMENTS

All photographs were taken specially for Conran Octopus by **Martin Brigdale** except the following:

Camera Press 11 ABOVE; **La Maison de Marie Claire** (*Santiago/Renault*) 11 BELOW, (*Pataut/Bayle*) 23 BELOW, (*Maltaverne/Faver*) 60 CENTRE and BOTTOM, 70 BELOW; **Cent Idées** (*Duffas/Lebeau*) 29 ABOVE, (*Duffas/Schoumacher*) 58–9, 62, 67 BELOW, 86, (*Maltaverne/Faver*) 60 TOP, (*Chabaneix/Garçon*) 66, (*Duffas/Lebeau*) 71; **Conran Octopus** (*Philip Dowell*) 13, 70 ABOVE, (*Grant Symon*) 87.